ISBN 978-1-5285-6617-9
PIBN 10065155

A WORKING MANUAL

—OF—

AMERICAN HISTORY

—FOR—

TEACHERS AND STUDENTS

—BY—

WILLIAM H. MACE

PROFESSOR OF HISTORY AND POLITICAL SCIENCE IN SYRACUSE UNIVERSITY,
AND EXAMINER IN HISTORY FOR HIGHER DEGREES TO THE
UNIVERSITY OF THE STATE OF NEW YORK

SYRACUSE, N. Y.
C. W. BARDEEN, PUBLISHER
1895

HOW TO USE THE MANUAL

The Thought of the Manual.—The idea underlying the Manual is that history is a process, and that it is not at all understood unless it is so conceived and studied. Fundamentally history is not an external or physical process. It is not a process of occurring events and incidents, although it has these accompaniments, but is rather the connected growth of ideas and institutions.

The Relation between Events and Ideas.—Ideas and institutions grow, but events do not. The former have a continuous existence, while the latter *only occur*. Events as such have no connection among themselves. They are the external forms in which ideas and sentiments, in the process of growth, express themselves. The physical facts of history are a means to the inner facts which are the end. This relation is often reversed in the mind of the student, by poor teaching. Not only is this relation reversed, but the student loses sight of the movement of ideas and the growth of institutions almost altogether, and constantly speaks in terms of events. The student must not form the habit of accounting for a series of events by referring to another series of external happenings. If he says that the Stamp Act caused the Stamp Act Congress, he may or may not be right. If this is all he can say, he has missed the point. If his mind passes directly from one of these acts to the other, the teacher ought to be alarmed. If events are to be accounted for, it must be done in terms of institutional ideas and sentiments. The event must be seen to flow out a wave of public sentiment or some thought, feeling or custom, which is its true cause, and its effects must be discovered in terms of a changed public sentiment. Now, the Manual is so constructed as to enable the teacher to preserve the proper relations between these two forms of historical phenomena, and also to force the student to explain movements in terms of institutional life.

Connections in History.—Turning to the growth of ideas and institutions, it may be said that here rests the true basis for viewing the subject-matter as a continuous process. Continuity is a law of life everywhere, but no where more than in history. Ideas and institutions in the process of growth not only move from one stage to another, and thus mark a sort of continuousness, but also, and more important still, they preserve in the new stage something of the old. This is illustrated in the fact that the growth of coöperation and union between the people of the thirteen colonies is found in every important event from 1760 to 1787, and that the sentiment and principle of nationality connects the great events from 1787 to 1870. This law of the continuous persistence of a great institutional idea is kept to the front not only in the Outline, but also in the Original Matter.

How Historical Progress is Marked. — In passing from one stage to another, ideas and institutions take on differences as well as retain a sameness. In fact the student becomes conscious of a new stage only by the discovery of differences in the ideas, sentiments, and purposes. The discovery of these differences suggest to the student the progress of institutional life, and when the difference becomes great enough to dominate the movement of events, the new stage has arrived, and the differentiation is marked enough to be designated as a new phase or period. The Manual does not follow the conventional division into periods and sub-periods. This is especially true of our history from 1760 to 1789, and from 1789 to 1870. The divisions made illustrate an effort to find and designate parts which will reveal the development of ideas and institutions according to the laws of growth. Over-lapping dates are put down because, under the laws of growth, ideas and movements over-lap. And instead of confusing the student, they ought to keep before his mind the very important fact that life is continuous, and is not broken up into sections, as so often illustrated by the artificial periods in some texts and in many outlines.

Historical Problems.—It appears from the above that the problem of history is the mastering of the process by which institutional life has come to be what it is. While institutional life exhibits the five great phases of politics, religious and moral influences, cultural agencies, industrial life, and social life, yet these all constitute one life and their unitary growth and inter-dependence prove it. Each phase or period of history is such by virtue of the fact that it is dominated by some characteristic movement. The problem of any period or sub-period is to discover and master that dominating movement. The answer to this problem the teacher must know from the beginning, in order that intelligent and definite direction may be given to the student's study. The student may not, perhaps should not, know in terms of the special problem what the solution will be. The Manual is constructed on the idea that there are definite and accurate problems in history which the student must work out himself, and that these range in importance from the mastery of the content of a single event, or a series, up through the meaning of sub-periods, and periods to the common content of our history as a whole.

Relative Value of Historical Matter.—When the teacher has discovered and solved the problem of any period or phase of institutional life, the question of the distribution of the student's time and energy is greatly simplified. An event, or any other fact, will have value to the student only in proportion to its contribution to the solution of the problem in hand. If it reveals little to the student, it is worth little. If it gives him great insight into the movement he is trying to master, it is an event of great value. By the same principle the least and the greatest event in a series can be determined. The amount of space given in a text to any fact is not a safe guide, and neither is the Outline intended to exhibit accurately the relative value of historical matter.

The True Guide in Historical Study.—As far as the subject-matter can set the purpose for which it is studied, the true guide in history will be found in the essence of the subject itself—its nature, principles and laws. Do not, therefore, slavishly follow the Outline and References. But hold to the leadings of the truth as revealed in the growth, and development of the life of the people. Drop out portions of the Outline if not needed or impossible of use by your grade of students, or extend it if not full enough. Do not try to read all the references. The large number of authorities is given to accommodate large classes, with but a short period each day devoted to the study, and to favor those communities where historical works are few.

The Way Found for Transfer of Old World Ideas and Institutions to the New World

General Causes Opening up America to Europe

General European Situation at the Close of the Middle Ages

1. Revival of learning and religion.
2. Widespread interest in commerce and navigation.
3. Remote and immediate causes of discovery of America discussed below.

The Effects of the Crusades

1. General intellectual results.
2. Special results pointing toward America.
   - (1) Improvements in navigation and shipbuilding.
   - (2) Travels in the East.
     - *a.* Visits of Marco Polo and Sir John Mandeville.
     - *b.* Work of others.

Portuguese Enterprise

1. How related to travels in the East.

3. Coast voyages and experiments with the compass.
4. Work of De Gama and others.
5. Direct and indirect relation to discovery of America.

Invention of Printing

1. Time and place.
2. General effect upon work of Columbus.

Political and Commercial Condition of Europe

1. Rise of great nations.
2. Ambitious and aggressive monarchs.
3. Fall of Constantinople.
   (1) Time and cause.
   (2) Effect upon overland trade with India.
   (3) Navigators go West and take employment with rival monarchs.
   (4) Need for a new route to India.

Christopher Columbus

1. Early preparation for his work.
2. How helped and hindered in Portugal.
   (1) By his marriage.
   (2) By aids to his growing idea.
   (3) By conduct of the state officials.
3. Aid from Spain.
   (1) Helps and hindrances.
   (2) His victory and conditions imposed.

4. The first voyage.
   (1) Experiences in reaching America.
   (2) Effects on Spain and rest of Europe.

Where European Nations Planted their Institutions

Ownership of Newly Discovered Lands Determined

1. By time of discovery.
2. By exploration and final settlement.

Spanish Explorations

1. Select for study only those events which
   (1) Extend Spanish claims
   (2) Or tend to confirm claims made.
2. Mark the limits on the map in each case.
3. Fix rightful, and also doubtful, claims as a whole.

Claims of the French—Treat in same way

Work of the English*

1. Study out same points as above.
2. Give more emphasis to English effort. Why?

---

*It is a common mistake, in dealing with European explorations, to assume that all explorers and events connected therewith belong to American history. Many of them belong to the history of the various nations, some to general history, some are of no historical value, while a few fall within the limits of American history, and only those whose influence affected to an appreciable extent the growth of American life.

Historical Geography of America*

2. Physical conditions.
   (1) Work out the general physical features of the continent having historical value.
   (2) Physical characteristics of each region.
      a. Work out those influencing life.
      b. State resemblances and differences between these regions.
      c. Draw conclusions in the light of this comparison.
3. The natives.†
   (1) A leading characteristics.
   (2) Raise the question of the extent to which they influenced American history.

References

For maratime revival, see general histories. Irving's Columbus; Columbus, by Charles Kendall Adams; Writings of Marco Polo and Sir John Mandeville; Goodrich's History of the Sea; Fiske's Discovery of America, i. 256–516, i. 1–212; Thwaite's Colonies; Fisher's Colonial Era; and Andrews' History of the United States Vol. 1.

Beazley's Henry the Navigator (maps and charts illustrating geographical knowledge from before Crusades to Columbus).

---

*Without doubt ideas are greatly influenced by physical environment. It does not follow however that all the geographical characteristics of America are to be studied as part of its history. A geographical fact becomes a part of history to the student only when he can trace the process by which it enters into the growth of human affairs, otherwise the fact is purely geographical.

†The story of the Indian and the Mound-builder is full of charm and appeals to the imagination. But the question still remains: Is this story a part of the history of American life?

The Planting of English Ideas and Customs and their Growth into American Institutions

Virginia, the Representative Southern Colony

A PERIOD OF PLANTING

The London and Plymouth Companies

1. Origin and nature.
2. Purpose—special and general.

The First Charter, 1606–1609

1. Parties to the Charter and the purpose of each.
2. Leading provisions.
3. Principal events.
   (1) Formation of the settlement and character of the colonists.
   (2) Work of John Smith.
4. Condition of the Colony in 1609.

Second Charter, 1609–1612

1. Cause; changes and their significance.
2. Leading events.
3. Changes in the laws.
4. Introduction of tobacco culture—effects.

Third Charter, 1612-1624

1. Changes in the new Charter and their influence.
2. Leading events.
   (1) New land tenure—effects.
   (2) Governor Yeardly and the First Assembly, 1619.
      a. Causes of both.
      b. Work and influence of both.
3. The labor system.
   (1) Indented servants.
   (2) Negro slaves; cause of introduction and effects.
4. Introduction of family life and its effects.
5. The written Constitution, 1621.
   (1) Origin and nature.
   (2) Results.
6. Loss of the Charter, 1624.
   (1) Causes in England and America.
   (2) Conduct of the Colony and its significance.
   (3) Effects upon the Colony.

References

Bancroft, i. 120-122; 138-137; 145-146 (old ed.). Bancroft i. 95-96 (Centenary ed.). Bancroft i. 84-133 (latest ed.). Lodge's English Colonies, 2-10. Doyle's English Colonies, i. 109-1[illegible] Fisher's Colonial Era, 30-48. Thwaite's Colonies, 65-75. C[illegible] tury Magazine, xxv. 69-83. Andrews' History of [illegible] States, i. 31-37.

DEVELOPMENT OF VIRGINIA'S POLICY TOWARD ENGLISH AUTHORITY

The King Wants the Tobacco Trade

1. Reasons.
2. Protest of Virginia and the result.

Governor Harvey and the Burgesses

1. Causes of the quarrel.
2. Action of the Burgesses and its significance.
3. King's decision and its effects.

Agitation for Restoration of London Co., 1631

1. Opposition of Virginians.
2. Account for the change of sentiment and study its significance.

The Commonwealth

1. State and explain Virginia's sentiment toward the Puritan revolution.
2. Parliamentary warships and commissioners.
3. Nature and meaning of the compromise. (Document I.)

Navigation Laws in Virginia

1. Nature and non-enforcement in Cromwell's time.
2. Under Charles II.

Grant to Arlington and Culpepper, 1675

1. Character of the grant.

2. Extent, significance, and results of the opposition.

Bacon's Rebellion. (Document II.)

1. Causes—specific and fundamental.
2. Leading events.
3. Results—fundamental and particular.
4. Does this rebellion mark the triumph of the movement discovered in the preceding events? Prove.

References

Bancroft, i. 197–207; 216–227 (old ed.); i. 153–159; 169–179; 531–558 (Centenary ed.) Doyle's English Colonies, i. 221–254. Lodge's English Colonies, 13–23. Bancroft, i. 135–149; 446–448; 455–474 (old ed.). Fisher's Colonial Era, 44–56. Cook's Virginia, 164–175; 193–199; 215–292. Thwaite's Colonies, 75–80. Andrews' History of the United States, i. 112–115.

TENDENCY OF DOMESTIC INSTITUTIONS

Virginia's Industrial System, 1624–1750

1. Its peculiarity. (Document V.)
2. Classes of laborers.
3. Results to the slaveholder.
   (1) Economical.
   (2) Social.
   (3) Political.
4. Results to the non-slaveholder.
   (1) Economical disadvantages.
   (2) Social.
   (3) Educational and political.

Social Life

1. Social grades and their causes.
2. Results of these distinctions.

Educational Facilities

1. Why no public schools in the South.
2. Attempts to found colleges.
3. Opportunities for education open
   (1) To slaveholder.
   (2) To non-slaveholder.

Religious Life

1. The Established Church.
   (1) How established.
   (2) To what extent supported by law?
2. The dissenters.
   (1) Who they were.
   (2) What disadvantages met them?

Politics

1. State government.
   (1) Legislation participated in by whom and from whence their authority?
   (2) Administration participated in by whom, and whence their authority?
   (3) Justice administered by what courts?
2. Local government.
   (1) County and parish systems.
   (2) Why no town government?
3. Account for government being controlled by the planters.

General Principle of Growth *

1. What law or tendency discovered in the development of Virginia's institutions?
2. Account for this tendency.

References

Lodge's English Colonies, 41–92. Doyle's English Colonies, i. 381–395. See topics above in contents of different editions of Bancroft. Fisher's Colonial Era, 56–61. Century Magazine, xxviii, 250–251; 853–865. Washington and His Country, 124–130. Gay's Madison, 49–51. Lodge's Washington, i. 15–28. Cook's Virginia, 364–374. Thwaites' Colonies, 96–111. Andrews, i. 119–122.

Massachusetts, the Representative New England Colony

A PERIOD OF PLANTING

Plymouth Company and Council †

1. Time and limits of the grants.
2. Motives of the parties.
3. Read story of first efforts to make settlements.

Pilgrims

1. Trace origin of Puritans.
2. Formulate their political and religious ideas.
3. Trace origin and history of Pilgrims to Plymouth.

---

* While these points touching institutional life belong to Virginia, they may be applied to the study of the Southern Colonies as a whole, with valuable results.

† The points under this head are not intended to reveal any phase of New England institutional life, but are merely introductory.

4. Work out resemblances and differences from Puritans.
5. Discover the principles in the Mayflower Compact.
6. Leading facts in the life of the Plymouth Colony.

References

Bancroft, i. 277–309 (old ed.); i. 210–243 (Centenary); i. 177–214 (last); Doyle, ii. 27–49. Lodge's Colonies, 341–342. Palfrey's New England, i. 101–160. Century Magazine, xxv. 351–355. Fisher's Colonial Era, 82–99. Campbell's Puritans in Holland, England, and America, i. 438–508; ii. 177–249. Thwaites' Colonies 113–124. Fiske's Beginnings of New England, 50–87.

The Massachusett's Bay Colony's Charter, 1629

1. Influences causing it.
2. Important points to be searched for:
   (1) Those revealing limits of the grant.
   (2) Those showing purposes, ostensible and real, of king and company.
   (3) Those indicating form, functions, and source of authority of the government.
   (4) Those indicating the rights of the settlers.
3. How and when the charter came to America.

The First Great Emigration to Massachusetts, 1629–1630

1. Relation to preceding events.
2. Leaders and numbers.

(2) Effects—immediate and remote.
(3) Contrast with Southern colonies.

Political Institutions Begin to Develop

1. Increase in the number of freemen.
   (1) Admitted on request, October, 1630.
   (2) Significance.
2. Suffrage conferred on church members.
   (1) An extension if compared with English law and with number indicated in the charter.
   (2) Significance of this qualification.
3. Beginnings of representation.
   (1) Causes—particular and fundamental.
   (2) How many representatives, and by whom chosen?
4. General Court establishes Town Governments, 1636.
   (1) Were any existing before 1636?
   (2) Nature and function of town meetings.
   (3) Effects—immediate and remote.
5. Local courts provided for.
   (1) Where did the charter locate judicial functions?
   (2) Significance.
6. Tendency toward popular rule.
   (1) Which events above reveal this? Prove.
   (2) Meaning of opposition to the rule of the Assistants.

(3) Significance of establishing annual elections.

(4) Proposition of the Puritan Lords and the significance of its rejection, 1636.

(5) Opposition to a permanent council, 1638.

References

Bancroft, i. 339–363 (old); i. 265–279; 283-288 (Centenary); i. 221–247 (last). Palfrey's New England, i. 287–293; 301–315; 353–355; 380–382; 434–435. Doyle's Colonies, ii. 90-94; 98–110. Lodge, 342–347. Fisher's Colonial Era, 100–114. Frothingham's Rise of the Republic, 16–17; 19; 24–25 (fine print). Hildreth, i. 179–190. Thwaites' Colonies, 124–129. Andrews' United States History, 1, 39–42. Fiske's Beginning's of New England, 88–106.

DEVELOPMENT OF POLICY TOWARD ENGLISH CONTROL AND IN DOMESTIC AFFAIRS

Nature of these Policies

1. To be discovered in the meaning of events and in the tendency of ideas.
2. Tendency in political affairs may be partly seen in above events.
3. Compare and contrast with tendencies in Virginia.

First Contest with English Authorities, 1634–1636

1. Nature and causes.
2. The trial and decision.
3. Results.

    (1) Attitude of Governor and Council.

(2) Ministers' resolutions.
(3) Military preparations.

Roger Williams, 1635–1636

1. His antecedents.
2. Causes of the controversy.
   (1) Attitude of England toward the colony.
   (2) Views and conduct of Williams.
      a. State them.
      b. Was he a Puritan?
      c. Does this age agree with Williams or his opponents?
3. Immediate results.
4. Meaning of the controversy.
   (1) Banishment voted by a small majority. Significance.
   (2) What if the people had voted on the question? Proofs and significance.
   (3) What does this differentation of ideas among Puritans prove?

Banishment of Mrs. Hutchinson, 1638

1. Political and religious causes.
2. Number of her sympathizers and its significance.
3. Did this controversy increase or decrease religous toleration?

Continuation of Immigration, 1634–1639

1. Causes—English and American.
2. Effects on England and Massachusetts.

The Body of Liberties, 1641

1. Origin.
2. Leading provisions. (Document III.)
   (1) Enumerate political doctrines.
   (2) State points pertaining to each institution.
3. General significance.

The New England Union, 1643

1. Causes in England and America.
2. Parties. Why no more?
3. Purpose and nature.
4. Results.

General Court divided into Two Houses, 1644

1. Original germs of the two houses.
2. Causes of the separation—particular and fundamental.
3. Results of the change.

References

Bancroft, i. 369–379; 416–422 (old). Bancroft, i. 293–300; 332–335; 339–342 (Cent.) Bancroft i. 249–262; 273–293 (last). Palfrey i. 390–422; 442–443; ii. 22–31. Doyle's Colonies, ii. 114–124. Lodge's Colonies, 346–352. Fiske's Beginnings of New England, 106–120; 140–162; Fisher's Colonial Era, 114–125. Thwaite's Colonies, 129–140; 154–157. Frothingham's Republic, 39–71. Straus's Roger Williams, 33–57. Andrews, i. 43–47.

Educational Influences

1. Massachusetts leaders college-bred.
2. Before 1642.
3. Compulsory education.
4. The act of 1647.
5. Harvard College, 1636.

6. Introduction of the printing press.
7. General meaning of these influences.
   (1) Relation to religion, politics and social life.
   (2) What relation to tendencies referred to above?

Authority of the Long Parliament in Question, 1646

1. Claim of Parliament.
2. Attitude of the General Court.
   (1) Toward Parliament's claim.
   (2) Toward a new charter.
3. General Courts reply to Parliament.*
4. Attitude of Cromwell.

The Quaker Invasion, 1656–1660

1, Origin and leading ideas of the Quakers.
2. Purpose and conduct in Massachusetts.
3. Action of the authorities.
   (1) The Union.
   (2) Massachusetts.
      a. Nature.
      b. Effects.
4. Attitude of the people. (Document IV.)
5. Causes and significance of repeal of laws against Quakers.

References

Bancroft, i. 451–459 (old); 363–370 (Centenary); 312–316 (last); Palfrey, i. 548–549. Doyle, iii. 88–93; 98–111. Lodge, 354–355. Fisher's Colonial Era, 146–148; 169–170. Thwaites' Colonies, 130, 188, 165–166. Fiske's Beginnings of New England, 179–198.

---

*Bancroft i. 307–308 (last) quotes the Court's and Winslow's statements. The latter states the principle contended for in the American Revolution down to 1776.

The Restoration

1. Attitude of Massachusetts toward Charles II.
2. King's orders to the General Court.
3. Royal Commissioners, 1664.
   (1) Purpose and action.
   (2) Conduct of the people.*
   (3) Significance.

Navigation Laws, 1660–1673. (Document VI.)

1. Recur to points in Virginia.
2. Laws of 1673—purpose, nature and effects.

Charter Taken Away, 1684

1. Causes—special and general.
2. Attitude of the Colony † and its significance.

Andros the Governor of New England, 1686–'89

1. The policy of James II.
2. Changes made by Andros and their meaning.
3. The revolution of 1688.
   (1) Work of Andros prepares for it.
   (2) Conduct of the people and its meaning.

The New Charter, 1692

1. Plymouth made a part of the Bay Colony.
2. Other changes made.
   (1) In the departments of government.
   (2) In qualifications for suffrage.

---

* Remonstrance addressed to the King is in Bancroft, i. 373–375 (last).

† The noble stand taken by the people is found in Bancroft, i. 404–406 (last).

The Salem Witchcraft

References

Frothingham's Republic, 77–83. Bancroft, i. 367–381; 395–406; 584–589; 599–601 (last). Lodge's Colonies, 389-392. Fisher's Colonial Era, 149–153; 157–164. Thwaites' Colonies, 166–169; 174–177. Andrews, i. 71–81. Fiske's Beginnings of New England, 242–278.

New England Institutional Life, 1630–1750

The View Taken

1. Based on similarity of insititutional ideas and their physical environment.
2. Do the facts point to the same or different principle of development in the different colonies? *

Industrial Life and Occupations

1. Make a list of leading occupations and compare with the South. (Document V.)
2. Which of these were favored by physical conditions?
3. Slave labor.
   (1) Did it flourish as in the South? Why?
   (2) In which section was the greater moral opposition? Prove.

---

* The tendency or principle of development ought to be known to the teacher from the beginning, but may not be discovered by the student till the series of events is done.

4. Commerce. (Document V.)
    (1) Leading exports and imports.
    (2) Relation to occupations and growth of population.

Social New England

1. Well defined classes.
2. Did the contrast increase or diminish? Meaning.
3. Home life and pastimes.
4. Other social occasions.
5. What the Puritan thought of amusements.

Culture Influences

1. Diffusion. Compare with the South.
2. The minister and his sermons.
3. Schools and colleges.
4. Papers and pamphlets.

Religion and Morality

1. The religious was the supreme sentiment.
2. The church organization and its political meaning.
3. The Puritan Sabbath.
4. Church services.
5. Intolerance and superstition.

Political Ideas and Organization

1. Is this the most democratic group? Prove.
2. Annual elections and their influence.
3. Town meetings.
   (1) Historical origin.
   (2) Nature of the organization.
   (3) Functions.
   (4) Effects—immediate and remote.
4. Judicial organizations and lawyers.

General Conclusions from Above Study *

References

See contents and index in Bancroft and Palfrey. Lodge's Colonies, 406–476. Thwaites' Colonies, 178–194. Fisher's Colonial Era, 313–320. Andrews, i. 92–97; 123–135. See contents in Fiske's Beginnings of New England.

The Middle Colonies

Institutionally Bridged the Chasm between New England and the South.

1. Developed little that was distinctive in institutions.
2. Diversity of population its greatest contrast.
   (1) Make a list of the elements in the population.
   (2) Draw conclusions from this list.

---

* It has been found helpful to compare New England and the South on the above points.

3. Variety in institutional life and habits was a dominant characteristic.
   (1) Each retained some old-world customs.
   (2) In this respect the middle colonies were more prophetic of the populations of our day than the other sections.

NEW YORK*

Voyages and Explorations of Hudson, 1609

1. Purpose.
2. Nature and results of his work.

Early Settlements

1. The Dutch traders, 1613
2. The Huguenots, 1623.
   (1) Cause of their coming
   (2) Compare with Puritans.
   (3) Their relation to New Amsterdam.
3. Fort Orange and others.

The West India Company, 1621

1. Nature of its Charter.

---

* This manual places emphasis on institutions, and finds the value of events in their contribution to institutional life. It hardly seems advisable to study in detail all the events of all the colonies. Such an attempt would likeiy prevent 'that careful investigation of some representative colony so necessary to give some idea of life-development.

2. Motives of the company.
3. Relation to settlements already made.

The Patroons and their System

1. Originated with the company.
2. The grants of land privilege.
3. Inducements to settlers.
4. Immediate and remote results of the system.
    (1) To the company.
    (2) To the settlement of the colony.
    (3) To the people of the state.

Progress of Events Under the Company

1. Early connections with the English.
2. Early relations with Indians.
3. A system of government established, 1626.
    (1) Leading features.
    (2) Relation to the people and its significance.
4. Rule of various governors up to Stuyvesant.
5. Introduction of slavery.
6. Trouble between Patroons and the company, 1640.
    (1) Causes—particular and fundamental.
    (2) The remedy and its significance.
7. Early struggle for political rights.
    (1) Cause.
        a. Nature of the governmental system.
        b. The rule of various governors.
        c. The example of the English.

(2) Kieft's Advisory Council.
a. Origin and functions.
b. Significance and results.
(3) The compromise in 1647.
(4) Appeal to Holland, 1650.
a. Grievances stated.
b. Results.
(5) The convention of deputies and Governor Stuyvesant, 1653.
(6) The company supports the governor.

8. Religious contests under Stuyvesant.
(1) The creed of the Dutch.
(2) Treatment of the Lutherans and Baptists.
a. Causes and character.
b. Attitude of the governor and company.
9. Relations with the Swedes.
10. Relations with the English colonies before the conquest.
(1) Plymouth, 1628 and 1633.
(2) Dutch post on the Connecticut.
(3) Emigrants from New England and Virginia.
(4) Dutch and English unite against the Indians.
(5) During Stuyvesant's rule.

The Conquest of New Netherlands, 1664

1. Causes and motives.
2. Terms and circumstances of the surrender.

3. Attitude of the colonists and its meaning.
4. Immediate results.
    (1) To the Dutch.
    (2) To the English colonies.
5. The reconquest and the restoration.

The Duke's Laws

1. Circumstances and causes.
2. Nature and purpose.
3. Effects.

The Duke's Grant

1. What it was.
2. How it affected New York.
3. Why Governor Nichols resigned.

New York Under Andros, 1674–1683

1. Relations with Connecticut and New Jersey.
2. The "bolting" act and the growth of New York city.
3. Religious sects and their relative importance.
4. Effects of the Navigation Laws.
5. Cause of recall of Andros.

Governor Dongon

1. Brings new political instructions.
2. The Charter of Liberties.
    (1) Source of authority under the charter.
    (2) Leading provisions.
    (3) Compare with Massachusetts's Body of Liberties.

3. The trouble with James II.
    (1) Why he revoked the charter.
    (2) Effects on the people.
    (3) Orders to Dongon.

The Revolution of 1688

1. Attitude of New York ; reasons.
2. Complications with Nicholson.

Jacob Leisler

1. Relations to Nicholson.
2. Relations to the militia.
3. Attitude of the council.
4. His work for the people.
5. Arrest and punishment.
6. Compare and contrast with Nathaniel Bacon.

Governor Sloughter

1. Instructions.
2. Reconstruction of the government.
    (1) Religious liberty except for Catholics.
    (2) A general assembly ; its acts.
3. Religious dispute between governor and assembly.
4. Expulsion of Catholic priests, 1700.

Growth of the English Church

1. Leading rivals.
2. Attempts of Andros to aid it.
3. Sloughter's instructions.
4. Quarrel between Fletcher and the Assembly.

(1) Questions in dispute.
(2) Results to the church.
5. Governor Cornbury's position.
(1) With reference to Presbyterians.
(2) On English acts of conformity.

The Struggle for Popular Government

1. Origin and progress under the Dutch.
2. Efforts under early English governors.
3. Effects produced by the Revolution of 1688.
4. Struggle between governors and assemblies.
   (1) Over annual appropriations.
   (2) Raising of taxes.
   (3) Over voting salaries.
5. Under Governor Bellomont.
   (1) His defense of Leisler and its significance.
   (2) Why he called a new assembly; its character.
6. Attitude of the assembly toward Governor Cornbury.
   (1) On salary and extravagances.
   (2) On expenditure of appropriations.
   (3) Factions united against the governor.
7. The Court of Chancery established.
   (1) Nature and purpose.
   (2) Opposition; cause and effect.
8. Liberty of the press secured, 1735.
   (1) The first newspaper in New York.
   (2) An opposition paper started.

(*a*) Attacks on the administration.
(*b*) Arrest of the editor.
(*c*) Why the defendant's lawyer came from Pennsylvania.
(*d*) The trial and its result.

9. Address of the assembly to Acting-Governor Clarke.
   (1) Absence of usual terms of flattery; significance.
   (2) Pledged not to raise large sums.
   (3) Asserted they would raise an annual revenue.

The Negro Plot

1. Origin of the delusion.
2. Punishment of the slaves.
   (1) Evidence and how obtained.
   (2) Number executed.
   (3) Compare with New England witchcraft.

The Institutional Life of New York

1. Politics and religion already studied.
2. Education.
   (1) Established under the Dutch.
   (2) Extent of the system.
   (3) Method of support.
   (4) Attitude of the English governors.
   (5) Compare and contrast with the schools of New England and the South.

3. Occupations and industrial life. (Document V.)
   (1) Leading ones and favoring physical conditions.
   (2) Domestic manufactures.
   (3) Foreign commerce.
      (*a*) With what countries.
      (*b*) Articles of exchange.
   (*c*) Relation to navigation laws. (Document VI.)

Social Life, 1700–1750

1. The basis of social distinctions in New York.
2. Compare and contrast English and Dutch settlers.
3. The degree of social separation.
   (1) Compare and contrast with New England and the South.
4. Pastimes of the various classes.

References

Bancroft, i. 475–527 (last edition). Fisher's Colonial Era, 177–173; 241–254. Lodge's English Colonies in America, 285–340. Thwaites' The Colonies, 186–207. Hendrick's Brief History of the Empire State, 10–83.

PENNSYLVANIA

The Grant to William Penn, 1681

1. Penn's interest in New Jersey Quakers, and its results.
2. Relations between the Penns and the Stuarts
3. Efforts to obtain a grant.

4 Limits.

5. Leading points in the charter.
   (1) Position and power of the governor.
   (2) Law-making body and its relations to the governor.
   (3) Law-making in its relation to the crown.
   4) Taxation.
      a. By local authorities.
      b. By English authority.
   (5) Religious toleration.

Penn's Letter

1. Preceded by a royal proclamation.
2. Addressed to people of the province.
3. Its political and religious sentiments.

Penn's Constitution, 1682

1. Drawn in England.
2. His idea of political freedom.
3. Relation between proprietor and governor.
4. Relation of the people to the council and assembly.

Large Emigration

1. From England.
2. From the continent.
3. Account for it.

The Assembly at Chester, 1682

1. Immediate cause and purpose.
2. Work of the meeting.

(1) Relation to the preceding documents.
(2) Position of the people of Delaware.
(3) Provisions relating to
a. Governor, council and assembly.
b. Religious freedom and Sabbath observance.
c. Capital crimes; compare with England and other colonies.
d. Jury trial; relation to Indians.
e. Peacemakers.
f. Offences against morality.
g. Inheritance; compare with other colonies.
h. Treatment of prisoners.

Penn's Opposition to Monopolies

1. Refuses to grant a monopoly of Indian trade between the Delaware and the Susquehanna.
2. Himself refuses an offer of revenue from exports on tobacco.

Treatment of the Indians

1. Penn's letter to them before coming over.
2. Recognition of Indians in making laws.
3. The great treaty.
   (1) Cause and nature.
   (2) Effects.
4. Compare and contrast with other colonies.

Growth and Variety of Population, 1685

1. Total population; account for it.

2. Variety.
    (1) English, Scotch, and Irish.
    (2) Germans, Swedes, and Finns.
    (3) Cause and effects.
3. Founding and growth of Philadelphia.

First Disturbance in the Colony

1. Departure of Penn for England.
2. Causes of the trouble.
3. Nature and meaning of the disturbance.
4. Immediate and remote consequences.

Separation of Pennsylvania and Delaware

1. Causes and leaders.
2. Results.

The Government Taken from Penn

1. The scism among the Quakers.
2. Imprisonment of Keith.
    (1) His offense.
    (2) Led to charge of persecution.
3. Fletcher made governor, 1693.
    (1) Appointed by the king; significance.
    (3) Delaware and Pennsylvania united.

Fletcher and the Assembly

1. Differences.
    (1) Assembly asserted old laws to be in force.
    (2) The governor asserts the royal prerogative.
    (3) Assembly refuse to re-enact its laws. Reasons.

(4) Assembly's manifesto calling for redress before voting supplies.

2. Effects.

Restoration of Penn's Authority, 1694

1. Difficulties in the way and how overcome.
2. Changes in the government made by the people.
   (1) The assembly.
      a. Sit on its own adjournment.
      b. Originate bills.
      c. Annually elected.
   (2) Biennial council.
3. Return of Penn.

Last Acts of Penn in the Colony, 1699–1701

1. New treaty with Indians.
2. Efforts against slave trade.
3. New constitutions.
   (1) For Pennsylvania.
   (2) For Philadelphia.
4. Returns to England to save the province.

The Struggle between the People and the Proprietary, 1700–1750

1. Generally between the assembly and the governors.
2. Questions in dispute under Evans, 1703–1709.
   (1) Reunion with Delaware.
   (2) Whether the governor could prorogue the assembly.

(3) Support of the war by the Quakers.
(4) The establishment of a judiciary.
(5) Right of impeachment by the assembly.
(6) Remonstrance to Penn.

3. Quarrel renewed under Governor Gookin.
   (1) Gookin's instructions.
   (2) Assembly arrests Logan.
   (3) His appeal to Penn.
   (4) Penn's reproof and threat.
      a. Nature and purpose.
      b. Result and its reason.
4. How Keith managed the assembly, 1718–1726.
   (1) Motives and policy.
   (2) Results and significance.
5. Quakers and war, 1739–1746.
   (1) Attitude of the Quakers toward Spanish war.
   (2) Means of forcing the governors to yield.
   (3) Rising opposition led by Franklin.
      a. Shown in King George's war.
      b. Also in French and Indian war.
      c. Results.

Institutional Life in Pennsylvania

1. Politics and government.
   (1) Nature seen in preceeding events.
   (2) Tendency was democratic.
   (3) Judiciary and its organization.
2. Religion and the church.

(1) Religious freedom.
(2) The various sects and their influence.

3. Education and schools.
   (1) Ignorance and superstition compared with other colonies.
   (2) Philadelphia's early schools.
      a. First school, 1683.
      b. First public school, 1689.
      c. Franklin's University, 1749.
   (3) Newspapers, literature, and science.
4. Society and the home.
   (1) Social classes; compared with other colonies.
   (2) Food and dress.
   (3) Houses and their furnishings.
   (4) Social gatherings and pastimes.
5. Industrial life and occupations. (Document V.)

References

Bancroft, i. 453–573 (last edition); ii. 24–31. Lodge's English Colonies in America, 211–272. Thwaites' Colonies, 235–220 Fisher's Colonial Era, 199–206; 260–271.

The Genesis of Common Ideas and Sentiments, 1760–1789

The Beginnings of Coöperation

INTER-COLONIAL WARS* AND CO-OPERATION, 1689–1760

King William's War, 1689–1697

1. Causes—immediate and remote.
2. Leading events—civil and military.
3. Effects.
   (1) Military knowledge gained by Americans.
   (2) Growth of coöperation.
      a. Events contributing to it.
      b. As affected by the treaty.

Queen Anne's War, 1702–1713

1. Causes—European and American.
2. Leading events—civil and military.
3. Effects.
   (1) Military experience.
   (2) Sentiment of coöperation.
   (3) Was the peace English or American made?

---

*Military events, as such, illustrate the art of war. They have historical significance only when their influence upon institutional growth is traced.

King George's War, 1744–1748

1. Causes—particular and general.
   (1) Which are American and which English?
   (2) Which are common to preceding wars?
2. Leading campaigns.
3. Results to America.

French and Indian War, 1755–1763

1. Causes—immediate and remote.
   (1) Are they mostly American or English?
   (2) Significance.
2. Leading events—civil and military.
3. Effects.
   (1) Particular.
      a. Make a list of those found in all the preceding wars.
      b. Number, character, and meaning of co-operative events.
      c. Compare the wars as to military experience.
      d. Financial and industrial on both America and England.
   (2) General.
      a. On political destiny of America.
      b. Religious and social ideas of America.

References

Bancroft, ii. 2 (last edition), see contents. Frothingham's Rise of the Republic, 84–94; 131–157. Andrews' History of the United States, i. 136–160.

BEGINNINGS OF ALIENATION AND UNION, 1700–1760

These Processes were Gradual and Simultaneous.

1. England convinced the colonies that her interests and theirs were not identical.
2. Parallel with the growth of this conviction arose the consciousness of common interests among the colonies.

Causes of the Above Movements

1. Growing divergence between American and English ideas.
   (1) Favored by geographical conditions. Prove.
   (2) Increased by social condition of the settlers.
   (3) Stimulated by study and self-reliant character developed in America. Show.
   (4) Aided by the greater political experience of all classes in America. Explain.
2. The attack on the American Charters.
   (1) Some changed before 1700.
   (2) New attacks on other colonies.
3. Quarrels with colonial governors.
   (1) Causes.
      a. Salaries. Why?
      b. Powers. Why?
   (2) Examples of the contest.
   (3) Attitude of England toward these conflicts and its effect.
4. Industrial and commercial restrictions.
   (1) Causes.

a. Fundamental–England's colonial theory.
b. Particular.—Demands of English trade.
(2) Leading restrictions on. (Document VI.)
a. Wool and woolen goods, 1699.
b. Hat trade and apprentices, 1719.
c. Pine tree reservation.
d. East India trade, 1721.
e. Sugar Act, 1733.
f. Iron and steel mills, 1750.
(3) Effects on
a. Relations between colonies and England.
b. Relations between the colonies.
c. Smuggling.

References

See contents and index to Lodge's, Thwaites' and Doyle's Colonies, and also to Fisher's Colonial Era, Bancroft's, Hildreth's and Andrews' histories.

Union Against England

THE STRUGGLE FOR THE RIGHTS OF ENGLISHMEN, 1760–1776

Leading Points in the Policy of George III.

1. Changes in colonial boundary lines.
2. Remodeling the charters.
3. Introduction of aristocracy.
4. Standing army.

5. Execution of navigation act.
6. Purpose of this policy.

Navigation Act ; Writs of Assistance, 1761

1. Causes.
   (1) Heavy debt.
   (2) Smuggling trade.
2. Nature and purpose.
3. Opposition in America ; reasons.
4. Speech of James Otis ; its principle. (Document VII.)
5. Effects on America.

References

John Adams' Works, i. 57–60. Bancroft, iv. 414–418 (old ed.) ; ii. 273–277 (Century ed.) ; ii. 546–548 (last ed..) Fiske's American Revolution, i. 12–13. Frothingham, 162, 168. Hart's Formation of the Union, 43–48. Hildreth, ii. 498–500 (rev. ed.). Hosmer's Samuel Adams, 40–45. Lecky's England in the 18th Century, iii. 328–330. Morse's John Adams, 24–25. Niles' Register, xiv. 137–140. Scott's Development of Constitutional Liberty, 237–246. Wells' Samuel Adams, i. 43–44.

Changes in the Navigation Act, 1763

1. Causes, immediate and remote.
2. Nature of act.
   (1) Smuggling punished by confiscation.
   (2) Navy used.
   (3) Naval, executive and judicial officers shared in spoils.
3. Effects.
   (1) On America.

a. Merchants memorialize assemblies, hold correspondence, and appeal to England.

b. Trade injured.

c. Common feeling against England and sympathy among American colonists.

(2) On England.

Stamp Act

1. New method of taxation. Reasons.
2. Purpose of England.
   (1) Immediate.
   (2) Indirect.
3. Effects on America.
   (1) Town meetings, mobs, and resignation of stamp officials.
   (2) Organizations.
      a. Sons and Daughters of Liberty.
      b. Merchant organizations. :
         a. Non-importation Society.
         b. Non-exportation Society.
      c. Consumers' organization: Non-consumption Society.
   (3) Meeting and work of colonial assemblies.
      a. Massachusetts.
      b. Virginia. (Document VIII.)
      c. New York.
      d. Others.

References

Atlantic Monthly, March 1888. John Adams' Works, i. 70–80. Annual Register (British), 1765, 18–21; 49–56. Bancroft, v. 91–92, 192–217, 269–280, 308–331 (old ed.); iii. 397–400, 417–436, 466–471, 491–506 (Centenary ed.); iii. 34–35, 60–62, 107–121, 131–148 (last ed.). Fiske's American Revolution, i. 14–18, 20–21. Frothingham, 161–184. Hart's Formation of the Union, 48. Hosmer's Samuel Adams, 46–54. Lossing's Field Book, ii. 671–674 (copy of Stamp Act); i. 460–464. Morse's John Adams, 26–32. Parton's Franklin, i. 459–463. Tyler's Patrick Henry, 57–79. Wells' Samuel Adams, i. 46–64. Wirt's Patrick Henry, 74–76 (Alta ed.).

Stamp Act Congress, 1765

1. Origin.
   (1) Prove it an outgrowth of preceding conditions.
   (2) Whence its authority?
2. Purpose, immediate and remote.
3. Work.
   (1) Read the documents issued. (Document IX.)
   (2) Enumerate the rights claimed.
   (3) On what ground did the colonists base their claim?
4. Effects of the congress.
   (1) Gave constitutional basis to opposition.
   (2) Unified sentiment and effort in America.

Repeal of the Act, 1766

1. Causes.
   (1) Influences in America.
   (2) English influences. (Document X.)

References

Andrews' History of the United States, i. 161–167. Atlantic Monthly, March, 1888. Annual Register (British), 1765, 18–21, 31–56. Bancroft, v. 91–92, 192–217, 333–336, 342–346, 363–372, 428–433 (old ed.); iii. 397–400, 417–436, 508–515, 519–524, 526–531, 570–573 (Centenary ed.); iii. 34–35, 60–62, 107–121, 149–214 (last ed.). Fiske's American Revolution, i. 14–18, 20–28. Frothingham, 161–200. Hosmer's Samuel Adams, 46–54, 78–89. Niles' Register, i. 12–14; ii. 337–355. Hart's Formation of the Union, 50–53. Hildreth, ii. 529–531. Tyler's Patrick Henry, 57–79. Parton's Franklin, i. 469–477, 478–482. Wells' Samuel Adams, i. 46–64, 106–109.

2. Effects.
   (1) Demonstrations of joy in England and America.
   (2) Declaratory resolves to save the principle in the new policy.

America's Gain

1. Value of union learned.
2. Moral sentiment aroused for standing by America against England. Significance.
3. American industry stimulated. How?

Tea Tax and other Measures, 1768

1. Tax on tea, paper, paints and glass.
2. Board of revenue commissioners.
3. Writs of assistance legalized.
4. Purpose of these measures.

Effects on America

1. Agitation and union.

(1) Sons of Liberty and Non-importation Societies again
(2) Industrial.
2. Massachusetts Circular Letter. (Document XI.)
(1) Nature and purpose.
(2) Effect on England; king commands:
a. Massachusetts to rescind letter.
b. Other assemblies to treat letter with contempt.
(3) America refuses obedience.
a. Massachusetts assembly votes not to rescind, 92 to 17.
b. Other assemblies vote to sustain Massachusetts.
c. Popular enthusiasm supports assemblies.

Non-importation Forces Changes.

1. First tea trick, 1770.
(1) Nature, aim and effects.
(2) Committees of correspondence formally organized, 1773.*
2. Tea trick number two, 1773.
(1) Nature and causes.
(2) Effects on America.

Boston Tea Party and Paul Revere's First Ride

1. Boston committee of correspondence; and how it organized opposition.

---

* Very important. Work out organization and operations.

2. The party. Dec. 16, 1773. (Document XII.)
   (1) Its invitations.
   (2) Work.
   (3) Paul Revere carries its compliments to New York and Philadelphia.
   (4) Significance of this event.

References

Andrews' History of the United States i. 167–170. Annual Register, 1768, 235–237; 1774, 58–67. Atlantic Monthly, April, 1888. Bancroft, vi. 100–107, 112–126, 143–147, 465–489 (old ed.); iv. 59–62, 69–74, 83–89, 271–281 (centenary ed.); iii. 251–252, 279–293; 443–458 (last ed.). Fiske's American Revolution, i. 28–84, 84–93. Frothingham, 208–230, 296–303, 303–311. Hildreth, iii. 24–32. Hosmer's Samuel Adams, 98–110, 153–159, 243–256. Lecky's England, iii. 380–406. Lossing's Field Book, i. 477–479, 481–488, 496–499. Wells' Samuel Adams, i. 142–144, 148–152; ii. 110–127.

England Strikes Back *

1. Boston Port Bill.
   (1) Cause and nature.
   (2) Effects, immediate and remote.
2. Other measures.
3. How the country stood by Boston. (Document XIII.)

First Continental Congress, 1774

1. Causes—particular and fundamental.
2. Make a list of its leading members.

---

* American Archives, ser. 4, i. 397–398 (address and covenant sent by the Boston committee to each town in the colony.)

Annual Register, 1774, 68–78, 233–236 (abstract of the bill; 239–240 (abstract of the Quebec bill); 1775, 2–22 (effects of these measures).

Work of the Congress

1. Purpose.
   (1 Cement union.
   (2) Redress of grievances.
2. Means to these ends.
   (1) Secret sessions.
   (2) Communication with Boston. (Documents XVI and XVII.)
   (3) Declaration of rights. Addresses to the king, people of England, people of Canada, and people of the colonies. (Documents XIV and XV.)
   (4) The association.
   (5) Show how each was a means.

Effects on America

1. Sentiment of union strengthened.
   (1) Constitutional basis more apparent.
   (2) Greater sympathy and more contributions for Boston.
2. Every colony voted to or did sustain its recommendations.
3. Militia organized and munitions of war collected. (Document XVIII.)

Effects on England (Document XIX.)

1. The King orders:
   (1) Governors to prevent appointment of delegates to next congress.
   (2) Governor Gage to enforce changes in Massachusetts charter.

2. On parliament.
   (1) Majority vote thanks to king for his measures.
   (2) Friends of America oppose it.
   (3) Lord Chatham, Jan., 1774, moves for conciliation.
   (4) Burke's motion and speech, March, 1775.
   (5) Petitions of business men to parliament.

References

Gentlemen's Magazine, 1774, 20–23, 25–27, 367–369, 570–571; 1775, 197–198, 199–200, 317–318, 360. Parliamentary History, xviii. 168–171, 179–181, 184–185. Parliamentary Register, i. 104–106, 116–117. John Adams' Works, i. 149–165. Annual Register, 1775, 23–36; 1774, 203–214, 218–224. Bancroft, vii. 126–135, 138–152 (old ed); iv. 353–361, 392–398, 401–411 (centenary); iv. 61–77 (last ed.). Curtis' Constitutional History, i. 6–17. Fiske's American Revolution, i. 100–111. Frothingham, 358–381. Hildreth, iii. 42–46. Hart, 59–68. Hosmer's Samuel Adams, 313–321. Journals of Congress, i. 19–23, 26–31, 46–49. Lecky's England, iii. 443–450. Morse's John Adams, 63–82. Tyler's Patrick Henry, 92–112. Wells' Samuel Adams, iii. 174–178, 213–248.

Lexington and Concord

1. Causes.
   (1) Enumerate fundamental ones.
   (2) List of the events operating as particular causes.
2. Alarming the country and arousing the Minute Men.
3. The fight itself.*

---

*Every student ought to read Bancroft's story of Lexington and Concord.

(1) Some characteristics.
(2) Historical significance.
a. Why did the Americans rejoice over the defeat of the British?
b. How many companies of Minute Men in the contest and what is its meaning? *
c. Meaning of size of army around Boston.
d. What was the effect of this conflict on the Americans' desire for their rights as Englishmen?
e. Effect on England.

Transition from Rights of Englishmen to Rights of Men

1. Leading events marking the beginning of the end of the first part of the revolution.
   (1) Lexington and Concord.
   (2) Bunker Hill and siege of Boston.
   (3) Ticonderoga.
   (4) King's proclamation.
   (5) Congress of 1775.
2. Union for rights of Englishmen a failure.
3. Union for rights of man now begins.

STRUGGLE FOR THE RIGHTS OF MAN

Origin and Growth of Independence

1. In the spirit of American institutions.
2. From New England union (1643) Americans accused of aiming at independence.

---

* See Bancroft.

3. Americans deny the charge.
4. Attitude toward independence while struggling for rights of Englishmen. (Document XVII.)
5. New England thought to be ready for it in 1774.*
6. Attitude of middle colonies, 1775.
7. The king promotes independence.
    (1) Refused to hear petition of congress of 1775.
    (2) Proclaimed colonists rebels.
    (3) Hired mercenary troops.
8. Movement begins in earnest.
    (1) Common sense, January, 1776. (Document XX.)
    (2) Action of colonial legislatures.
        a. North Carolina instructs for independence, April, 1776.
        b. South Carolina makes a new government. Significance.
        c. Rhode Island disclaims allegiance, May 4.
        d. Virginia's convention instructs delegates for independence and votes a declaration of rights of man, May 15.
    (3) Action of congress.
        a. Richard Henry Lee moves for independence, in June.
        b. Vote postponed. Reasons.

---

* See Morse's John Adams, 53–69.

c. First vote, how secured?

d. Jefferson the author and John Adams the defender of the declaration.

9. Political doctrines of the declaration.* (Document XXI.)

(1) Sets forth rights of men.

(2) Relations with England and incidentally relations between the states.

References

Andrews, i. 171–180. Annual Register, 1775, 120–125. Bancroft, vii. 148–150, 182–185, 228–232. 271–277 (old ed.); v. 257–262 (Centennary ed.) Frothingham, 153–157, 174–175, 198–200, 244–248, 290–293, 400–402. Gentleman's Magazine, 1775, 195–201. Hart's Formation of the Union, 70–80. Hildreth, iii. 50–56, 65–67 (revised ed.). Lossing's Field Book, ii. 67–70. Morse's John Adams, 53–77. Roosevelt's Gouverneur Morris, 28–52. Scott's Constitutional Liberty, 290–297. Stevens's Sources of the Constitution of the United States, 25–39.

Leading Military Events

1. First year of war (April, 1775, to April, 1776), mainly a series of victories for Americans.
2. Disaster on Long Island and retreat up the Hudson and across the Jerseys, Aug. to Dec., 1776.
3. Great victories at Trenton and Princeton, defeat at Brandywine and loss of Philadelphia, Christmas, 1776, to Sept., 1777.
4. Burgoyne's invasion and surrender.

---

* The doctrinal portion of the declaration should be analyzed and its principles stated.

5. War in the South.
   (1) Its partisan character.
   (2) Its great events: Camden, King's Mountain, Cowpen's and Greene's campaign.
6. Event's which made the Mississippi our western boundary-line.
7. Yorktown and treaty of peace.

References: for battles

Andrews, i. 181-222. Bancroft. Carrington's Battles of the Revolution. Fiske's American Revolution i. and ii. Hildreth. Lecky's England. Lodge's Washington. Lossing's Field Book. Marshall's Washington. Parton's Franklin. Roosevelt's Winning the West.

For Treaty

Annual Register, 1783, 339–42. Bancroft vi. 183-192 (Centenary ed.). Burnet's Northwest Territory, 75–82. Dunn's Indiana, 131–151. Fiske's Critical Period of American History, 17–36. Hart's Formation of the Union, 95–98. Hildreth, iii. 411–420. Hinsdale's Old Northwest, 153–160. Journals of Congress, iv. 323–325. Lecky's England, iv. 271–84. Marshall's Washington, ii. 39–40. Morse's John Adams, 198–240.

Results of the Revolution

1. Political and governmental.
2. Religious and moral.
3. Industrial and financial.
4. Social.

Growth toward a Permanent Basis of Union

STATE SOVEREIGNTY AS THE BASIS OF UNION

Origin of State Sovereignty

1. The colonial situation favored it. Prove.

2. Necessity, in the revolution, for a principle of union.
   (1) Appears in early meetings of the Continental Congress.
   (2) In discussions over internal questions.
   (3) Recognized in Franklin's plan of a confederation.

Origin of the Confederation

1. Relation to the war of the revolution.
2. Relation to the Declaration of Independence.
3. Struggle over the articles in congress, 1776–1777.
   (1) Questions at stake.
   (2) Changes made in the first draft and their significance.
   (3) Method of adoption and its meaning.
   (4) Delay in adoption ; causes.

Nature of the Confederation as Revealed in the Articles

1. Nature and significance of the second article.
2. From a study of the remaining articles, what conclusion may be reached?
   (1) As to the general nature of the confederation.
   (2) As to the relative amount of power of the states and the congress over foreign questions.

(3) As to their relative amount of power over internal or domestic questions. Cite proof of each.

3. Proof that this distribution of power harmonizes with the causes and circumstances that produced the confederation.

Defects of the Articles

1. A list of the defects.
2. The fundamental defect discovered and its origin explained.
3. Could this defect have been avoided by the makers of this instrument? Reason for the answer.

Events bearing on the Decline of the Confederation

1. Discontent in army at close of the war.
2. Condition of congress.
3. Industrial situation.
4. America's reputation abroad.
5. Shay's rebellion.

References

Andrews' History of the United States, 223-229. Bancroft's History of the United States, v. 10-15, 199-208, 283-284; vi. 59-86, 136-153, 167-176 (new ed.); ix. 436-451 (old ed.); v. 345-353 (Centenary). History of the Constitution, 45-53, 59-77, 137-140, 147-153, 167-176. Cyclopedia of Political Science, i. 574-577. Curtis, Constitutional History, i. 104-114, 127-134, 186-195, 208-220, 225-226. Dawson's Federalist, 90-100. Elliott's Debates, i. 67-78; v. 110-112. Fiske's Critical Period, 105-113, 142-151, 167-178, 179-186, 208-213; Failure of American Credit after the Revolutionary War (*see* Atlan. 58 : 77-88); the Paper Money Craze of

1786 and Shay's Rebellion (*see* Atlan. 58: 376–385); Weakness of the United States Government Under the Articles of Confederation (*see* Atlan. 57: 577–589). Gay's, Madison, 76–87. Hart's Formation of the Union, 103–117. Hildreth's History of the United States, iii. 395–400, 421–422, 430–437, 450–454. Von Holst's Constitutional History, i. 19–30, 39-46. Hosmer's Samuel Adams, 465–465. Jefferson's Writing's, i. 26–36, 78–79, 406–407, 413–414, 389-392, 518; ii. 105–106. Lossing's Field Book, i. 672–676. Shay's Rebellion (*see* Harper, 656–662). McMaster's History of the United States, i. 130–138, 177–185, 223–226, 255–259, 300–330. Marshall's Washington, ii. 9–37, 41–56; 94–97. Pitkin's History of the United States, ii, 154–178. Rives' Madison, i. 253–266, 382–408, 547–548; ii. 47–51 (notes), 164–180. Schouler's History of the United States, i. 14–17. Story's Commentaries on the Constitution, i. 157–162, 168–172. Edward Stanwood's A Glimpse at 1786 (*see* Atlan. 57, 777–788). Wells' Samuel Adams, 211, 222–243. Walker's Making of the Nation, 1–20. Western Annals, 280–283.

GROWTH OF NATIONAL SOVEREIGNTY AS THE BASIS OF UNION

This Form of Union is the Second Phase of Domestic Union.

1. Germs of nationality parallel in time with state sovereignty.
2. Many events under the confederation have a double content, pointing back to state sovereignty and forward to nationality.*

Expressions of National Sentiment

*In interpreting the events under the confederation the student gets the whole content or meaning only when he views events in the light of both their causes and effects.

1. Christopher Gadsden in the Stamp Act Congress.
2. Patrick Henry in congress of 1774.
3. Tom Paine in "Common Sense", Jan., 1776.
4. Edward Rutledge, tired of the debates over the confederation, wrote that he was ready to "propose . . . a special congress . . . of new members" for the purpose of making a new government.

New York and New England Move.

1. Representatives of New England in convention at Boston, 1780.
2. Convention at Hartford, Nov., 1780.
   (1) New England and New York represented.
   (2) Urged congress to act.
   (3) Sent a circular letter to all the states on the defects of the confederation.
   (4) Proceedings sent to other states, to Washington and congress.

Early Work of Hamilton

1. Elaborated for Robert Morris the plan of a national bank, 1780.
2. Great letter to Duane, 1780. (Document XXII.)
3. In April, 1781, he sent to Morris the charter and plan for a national bank to be incorporated by congress.
4. Published the *Continentalist*, 1781–1782.

Washington's Early Efforts to promote a Strong Government

1. As commander-in-chief he soon felt the need of a more centralized government.
2. Many recommendations to the continental congress pointed toward it.
3. In private letters to members he urged the exercise of more power by congress.
4. Similar views set forth in correspondence with governors and influential men in the states.
5. The Newburgh address and how it was met.
6. Circular letter to the governors, June, 1783.
   (1) Leading points.
   (2) Effects on the country.

Cessions and Government of Western Territory, 1781–1787

1. Cessions and their significance.
2. Origin, nature and purpose of Ordinance of 1787.

The Interests of Commerce Point the Way to a more Perfect Union.

1. England's injury to our commerce; causes and effects.
2. Washington, Jefferson and Madison interested in developing intercourse with the West.
3. Recommended coöperation with Maryland.

Virginia and Maryland Act.

1. Meeting at Alexandria and Mount Vernon.
   (1) Commissioners meet March, 1785.
   (2) Jurisdiction of Potomac and Chesapeake settled.
   (3) Common commercial regulations for all discussed. Significance.
2. Maryland legislature adopts report and suggests that Delaware and Pennsylvania join them in a set of trade regulations.
3. Virginia calls a great trade convention.

Annapolis Convention, 1786

1. Delegates from five states.
2. Leading men.
3. Why another convention was called.
4. Hamilton's report amended, adopted and sent to congress and the states represented.
5. How the report was received.
   (1) By the state legislatures.
   (2) By congress.

References

Andrews' History of the United States, i. 230–234. Bancroft's History of the United States, vi. 182–185, 195–197 (new ed.); History of the Constitution, 195–203 Curtis's Constitutional History, i. 186–195. Eliot's Debates, v. 96–97. Fiske's Critical Period, 211–218. Gay's Madison, 47–63. Hart's Formation of the Union, 118–119. McMaster's History of the United States, i. 277–279, 389–390. Madison's Papers, ii. 694–707. Marshall's Washington, ii. 105–109. North American Review, liii: 320; 122: 29. Rives' Madison, i. 548–552; ii. 57–59, 97–102, 126–130, 132–137. Story's Commentaries on the Constitution, i. 188–190.

The Constitutional Convention, 1787

1. How it was called.
   (1) Resolutions of states.
   (2) Why congress and certain states came to support the call.
2. Delegates.
   (1) How appointed and their instructions.
   (2) List of the leading ones and their fitness.
3. The Virginia plan of a constitution. (Document XXIII.)
   (1) Origin.
   (2) Leading ideas and fundamental principle.
   (3) Lack of harmony between this plan and instruction to delegates. Significance.
4. The New Jersey plan. (Document XXIV.)
   (1) Its origin.
   (2) Leading ideas and dominant principle.
   (3) Contrast with Virginia plan.
5. Hamilton's plan. (Document XXV.)
   (1) Origin and nature.
   (2) Purpose of its author.
6. Discussions over these plans.*
   (1) The parties developed and their basis.
   (2) The danger and significance of their contests.
7. The Connecticut Compromise. (Doc. XXVI.)

* The teacher in directing the study of these debates must be guided by the maturity of the class and the general purpose of the course.

(1) Origin, nature, and meaning.
(2) Effects on the small states.

8. The contest over slavery.
   (1) Representation and direct taxation.
      a. Origin and clause.
      b. The compromise and significance.
   (2) The African slave trade.
   (3) The fugitive slave clause.
9. Creation of the executive. (Document XXVII.)
   (1) Plans proposed.
   (2) Methods of election and tenure of office.
   (3) Relation to other departments.
10. The national Judiciary.
   (1) Plans and methods.
   (2) Relation to other departments.*
11. Final work of the convention. (Document XXVIII.)

References

Andrews' History of the United States, i. 234-239. Bancroft's History of the United States, vi. 198–367 (new ed.); History of the Constitution, 207–269, 326–374. Curtis's Constitutional History, i. 256–348, 368–421, 563–640. Fiske's Critical Period, 220–268, 277–305; The Federal Convention (*see* Atlan. lix: 225–240). Gay's Madison, 88–97, 98–114. Greeley's American Conflict, 43–49. Hart's Formation of the Union, 121–128. Hamilton's Works, ii. 395–409. Hildreth's History of the United States, i. 482–503. Lodge's Hamilton, 60–65; Washington, 27–38, 438–470. McMaster's History of the United States, i. 438–451. Madison's Papers,

* After reading the debates and studying the relations between departments, the principles controlling the convention in distributing functions and in creating departments ought to be stated.

ii. 728–746. Marshall's Washington, ii. 110–125. Parton's Franklin, ii. 564–584. Pitkin's History of the United States, ii. 224–264. Rives' Madison, ii. 272–329, 343–353, 359–509. Roosevelt's Gouverneur Morris, 129–168. Stevens' Sources of the Constitution, 41–58. Schouler's History of the United States, i. 36–47. Wilson's Rise of the Slave Power in America, i. 40–56. Walker's Making of the nation, 21–50.

Ratification of the Constitution *

1. Method and its significance.
2. Public sentiment as seen in
   (1) Wild rumors among the people.
   (2) Action of congress.
   (3) Attitude of Samuel Adams, Patrick Henry, Richard Henry Lee, George Clinton, and Luther Martin.
   (4) Merchants, professional men, and tories.
   (5) The Federalist, Letters from a Federal Farmer, and in other controversial writings.
3. Would the people, voting directly and immediately, have ratified the constitution? Reasons.

Ratifying Conventions, 1787–1790

1. In the small states.
   (1) Some unanimously.
   (2) Others by large majorities.
   (3) Account for such favorable action.

---

*The teacher may use much or little of the matter on ratification. It deserves more attention than it generally gets, if, for no other reason, to correct the false conception of most Americans as to origin of our constitution.

2. The battle begins in Pennsylvania.
    (1) Contest in the legislature.
    (2) Campaign for election of delegates.
    (3) Debates in convention. (Document XXIX.)
        a. Opponents and their arguments.
        b. Wilson's defence of the constitution.
        c. The vote and its effects.
3. The first doubtful convention in Massachusetts.
    (1) Position of Massachusetts past and present.
    (2) Conflicting interests and the compromise.
        a. How it was accomplished.
        b. The amendments and their effects.
4. Virginia convention, June, 1788.
    (1) Campaign began early.
    (2) People from all parts of the state at the convention.
    (3) Make a list of opponents and friends.
    (4) Patrick Henry's arguments. (Document XXX.)
    (5) Effects of the victory.
5. The fight in New York, June, 1788.
    (1) Conduct of New York delegates at Philadelphia. Meaning.
    (2) Leaders on each side and their work.
    (3) Effect of Virginia's ratification on the convention.
    (4) Madison's letter to Hamilton; its significance.
    (5) The compromise; its cause, nature, and danger.

(6) Tardy states, reasons.

The Struggle for a Bill of Rights

1. Why the convention did not put one into the constitution. (Document XXXI.)
2. Why a great cause of opposition to ratification.
3. Opponents of the constitution organize for another constitutional convention. Reasons.
4. Friends of the constitution favor congressional amendment.
   (1) Reasons.
   (2) Washington's recommendation.
   (3) Madison's amendments.
5. The first ten amendments passed and ratified.
   (1) Effect on opponents of the constitution.
   (2) Real end of the campaign for the constitution.
   (3) Greatly influenced the administration of whole constitution.

General Results of the Movement for a More Perfect Union

1. State sovereignty demonstrated its radical weakness as a basis of union.
2. Every step taken indicated a rise in the sentiment of nationality.*

---

* The meaning of this statement is not comprehended unless this sentiment has already been seen in the movements before the convention, in the work of the convention itself, in each ratifying convention, in the first ten amendments, and in other minor events.

3. The constitution was a moderate triumph of nationality.
4. Beginnings of the differentiation of political ideas.
5. Germs of political parties deposited.

References

Andrews' History of the United State, i. 239–240. Bancroft's History of the United States, vi. 371–460 (new ed.); History of the Constitution, 381–460. Elliot's Debates, ii. (Mass. and N. Y.): iii. (Va.). Fiske's Critical Period, 317–344. Gay's Madison, 115–127. Hart's Formation of the Union, 128–135. Hammond's Political History, i. 19–29. Von Holst's Constitutional History, i. 60–61; Constitutional Law, 25–26. Hosmer's Samuel Adams, 392–401. Jefferson's Writings, i. 79–82, 318, 329, 355; ii. 316, 318, 358, 375, 399 (old ed.). McMaster's History of the United States, i. 454–490. Magruder's Life of Marshall, 50–87. Rives' Madison, ii. 520–558, 560–612, 624–647. Stevens' Gallatin, 34–41. C. E. Stevens' Sources of the Constitution of the United States, 207–248. Schouler's History of the United States, 52–70. Tyler's Patrick Henry, 279–301. Walker's Making of the Nation, 41–62. Wells' Samuel Adams, iii. 254–269. Wirt's Life of Patrick Henry, 263–308.

GROWTH OF NATIONALITY, 1789–1870

Nationality and Democracy, 1789–1840

STRUGGLE BETWEEN NATIONALITY AND STATE SOVEREIGNTY, 1789–1820

Nature of this Struggle

1. Preceding conflicts between these two ideas and sentiments.
2. The last great contest for state sovereignty as such.

Condition of the Country in 1789

1. Geographic extent.
2. Population and its distribution.
3. Industrial situation.
4. Education and its agencies.
5. Political situation.
   (1) What the revolution had not accomplished.
   (2) Germs of political parties.
   (3) Fundamental ideas.

Organization of the Government

1. Elections, congressional and presidential.
2. First inauguration.
3. Formation of cabinet and judiciary.

Leading Measures and Events of Washington's Administration, 1789–1797

1. Financial.
   (1) Tax on imports and touage.
   (2) Funding and Assumption bills.
   (3) Excise bill.
   (4) United States bank.
   (5) Effects of these measures.
2. Foreign relations.
   (1) With France. (Document XXXII.)
   (2) With England.

References

Andrews' i. 243–272. Bolles' Financial History of the United States, ii. 22–155. Gay's Madison, 202–215. Hamilton's Report on Manufactures. Hart's Formation of the Union, 85–163. Hildreth's History of the United States, i. 152–174, 206–215, 253–262, 411–440, 481–497. Von Holst's Constitutional and Political History, i. 80–118. Jefferson's Writings, iii. 154–163; also index to iii. and iv. Johnston's History of American Politics. Lalor's Cyclopedia of Political Science, *art.* Bank Controversies (Alexander Johnston) i. 199–204. Lodge's Alexander Hamilton, 86–184; George Washington, ii. 110–120, 139–206. McMaster's History of the People of the United States, i. 568–584; ii. 25–41, 89–142, 165–188, 246–284. Marshall's Life of George Washington, ii. 178–190, 255–384. Morse's Thomas Jefferson, 97–102, 111–123, 146–160. Niles' Weekly Register, v. 153–228. Pitkin's History of the United States, ii. 317–420, 442–478. Rives' Life of Madison, iii. 1–28, 67–118, 139–188. State Papers, i. 46. Schouler's History of the United States, i. 86–93, 130–142, 158–162. Stevens' Albert Gallatin, 256–288. Walker's Making of the Nation, 62–136.

Decline of the Federalist Party

1. Trouble with France.

(1) Demands of the Directory.
(2) Treatment of American ministers.
(3) Gives Federalists large majority in congress.

2. Alien and Sedition laws.
(1) Purpose and nature.
(2) Immediate consequences.
(3) Kentucky and Virginia resolutions, 1789–1799. (Document XXXIII.)

3. Internal dissensions and defeat in 1800.

Anti-Federalist Party and its Work

1. Its fundamental principle.
2. Leader and organizer.
3. Attitude toward questions since 1798.
4. Triumph in 1800.
(1) Causes and significance.
(2) Character of the campaign.
(3) Disputed election; dangers and effects.
(4) Jefferson's inaugural. (Document XXXIV.)
5. Purchase of Louisana, 1803.
(1) Causes—fundamental and particular.
(2) Political questions involved.
(3) Immediate and remote consequences.
6. Carrying out campaign pledges.
(1) Modification of the judiciary.
(2) Cutting down expenditures.
(3) Internal taxes.
(4) Social and other changes at Washington.
(5) Effects on both parties.

7. Foreign policy and relations.
   (1) England's aggressions—their causes, nature and effects.
   (2) America's response.
      a. Jefferson's gunboats and negotiations.
      b. Non-intercourse.
      c. Embargo.
   (3) Political and commercial effects of these acts.

References

Andrews' i. 275–281, 305–314, 325–340. Adams' John Randolph, 27–37, 56–74, 83–94, 123–190. Brougham's Historical Sketches of Statesmen, iii. 280–290. Gay's Madison, 240–300. Hart's Formation of the Union, 164–189. Hildreth's History of the United States, ii. 36–44. Von Holst's Constitutional and Political History, i. 138–226. Jefferson's Writings, iv. and v. index. Johnston's History of American Politics, 40–68; Representative American Orations, i. 99–116, 203–227. Lalor's Cyclopedia of Political Science, *art.* Anti-Federal Party (Alexander Johnston), i. 99–100; *art.* Democratic-Republic party (Alexander Johnston) i. 768–772. Lodge's Alexander Hamilton, 194–236. McMaster's History of the People of the United States, ii. 308–323, 367–451, 497–537; iii. 1–45, 198–210. Morse's Thomas Jefferson, 193–218, 231–253, 259–268. Morse's John Quincy Adams, 37–69. Schouler's History of the United States, i. 480–488; ii. 1–7, 37–52, 75–111, 158–165. Schurz's Henry Clay, i. 67–74. Sumner's Jackson as a Public Man, 27–29. Walker's Making of the Nation, 137–213.

The War of 1812

1. Condition of the country, 1810–1812.
   (1) Physical resources.
   (2) Intellectual and moral resources.

2. Causes of the war—immediate and remote.
3. Position of parties and sections.
   (1) Opposition to declaration of war. Reasons.
   (2) Conduct of opposition in congress.
   (3) Opposition in New England * and elsewhere. (Document XXXVI.)
4. Leading events of the war.
   (1) On the water.
   (2) On land.
   (2) The treaty and its meaning.
5. Results of the war.
   (1) Political.
      a. Position of the Federalists. Why?
      b. Condition of the Republican party. Why?
      c. Era of good feeling; fundamental cause.
      d. Has liberal construction gained or lost? Meaning. (Document XXXV.)
   2. International.
      a. The questions causing war.
      b. The Monroe Doctrine—origin, nature, and significance, 1823. (Document XXXVII.)
   (3) Financial and industrial.
      a. War debt.
      b. United States Bank re-chartered, 1816. Why now and not in 1811?

---

* Make a list of the recommendations and resolutions of the Hartford convention. What political principle are they based on? Compare with Kentucky and Virginia resolutions.

c. Foreign trade and home production.
d. Danger of peace to American production.
e. Tariff of 1816—authors, purpose, and effects.
f. Internal improvements, origin, growth, and political and industrial significance, 1808–1820.

The Triumph of First Phase of Nationality

1. The events making this result.
2. Connection between the war and this result.

References

Andrews' i. 282–304, 315–324. Benton's Thirty Years' View, 1–16, 21–23, 32–34. Blaine's Twenty Years of Congress, i. 178–192. Gay's James Madison, 283–320. Hart's Formation of the Union, 191–258. Hildreth's History of the United States, iii. 196–206, 232–237, 242–247, 262–323, 581–592. Von Holst, Constitutional and Political History, i. 200–277, 396–423. Johnston's History of American Politics, 69–81. Lalor's Cyclopedia, of Political Science, *art.* Hartford Convention (Alexander Johnston) i. 624–626; *art.* Embargo (Alexander Johnston) ii. 81–85. Lodge's Daniel Webster, 61–66, 156–171. McMaster's History of the People of the United States, iv. 1–600. Madison's Works, ii. 186–187, 196, 206, 215, 290–349, 404–405, 407–427, 429–431, 439, 451, 455–458, 464–465, 488, 523–524, 536–538. Morse's John Quincy Adams, 37–69, 130–137. Niles' Weekly Register (see topics in index of vols. 1–25. Schurz's Henry Clay, i. 62–66, 77–85, 88–97, 126–171, 209–210. Schouler, ii. 381–462, and index. Walker's Making of the Nation, 214–273.

NATIONALIZATION OF DEMOCRACY, 1812–1840

A New Phase of Nationality

1. The plain people develop a deeper interest and action in national affairs.

2. Strengthens the sentiment of union.

Campaign of 1824

1. Old parties disintegrated and new ones not organized.
2. Leading candidates; effect on the people of each section having a candidate.
3. Failure of congressional caucus; significance.
4. No choice by electors; Adams elected by the House.

Election of Jackson and the Triumph of the People, 1828

1. Campaign opens in 1825.
2. Leading arguments.
   (1) That congress had violated the democratic principle in electing Adams. Significance.
   (2) That Adams and Clay secured Jackson's defeat by corrupt bargain.
   (3) That Jackson was a man of the people while the others represented an office-holding aristocracy. Significance.
3. New campaign methods.
4. Results as interpreted by
   (1) Scenes at the inauguration.
   (2) By the events which followed.

New Kind of President

1. Jackson's antecedents and their meaning.

2. His conception of his position as president and its meaning.

New Kind of Constituency

1. Position of leaders and their followers before this period.
2. Leaders and people assume new attitude toward the national government.
   (1) This new condition marks greatest revolution since adoption of constitution.
   (2) Beginning of second phase of nationality.
   (3) These new conditions account for many succeeding movements.

New Civil Service Policy

1. Principles and practice of Jackson's predecessors.
   (1) Washington's rules and favorable conditions.
   (2) John Adams and the midnight appointments.
   (3) Jefferson's problem and how he solved it.
   (4) John Quincy Adams the ideal civil service reformer.
2. First "clean sweep".
   (1) Causes found in preceding events.
   (2) Effects; immediate and remote.

References

Andrews' i. 348–362. Benton's Thirty Years' View, i. 111–114, 159–163. Von Holst's Constitutional and Political History, ii. 1–27. Johnston's History of American Politics, 96–101, 105–106.

McMaster's History of the People of the United States, ii. 585–588. Morse's John Quincy Adams, 179–181, 201–205. Niles' Weekly Register, index to Vols. 25–36. Roosevelt's Thomas H. Benton, 69–87. Schouler's History of the United States, iii. 409–420, 426–440, 451–465. Schurz's Henry Clay, i. 204–257, 332–337. Shepard's Martin Van Buren, 38–48, 89–99, 177–183. Sumner's Andrew Jackson as a Public Man, 73–99, 108–118, 139–148. Woodrow Wilson's Division and Reunion, 19–34.

New Phase of State Sovereignty begins to Appear

1. Preceding public expression of this principle.
2. Nullification by South Carolina.
   (1) Calhoun's "South Carolina exposition," 1828.
   (2) Webster-Hayne debate, 1830.
   (3) Calhoun's "Address to the people of South Carolina," 1831.
   (4) State convention passes
      a. ordinance of nullification, 1832.
      b. Action of state legislature.
3. Action of national authorities.
   (1) Jackson's proclamation. (Doc. XXXVIII.)
   (2) Force bill and compromise tariff.
4. Fundamental cause of controversy.
5. State sovereignty becomes a means of protecting slavery.*

New Financial Policy

1. The bank controversy.

---

* It is important to note this change. To Jefferson and Madison state sovereignty was a noble principle, but in its later development it is a shield to slavery.

(1) Causes—particular and fundamental.
(2) A leading issue in 1832.

2. Bank charter vetoed and deposits removed.
3. Financial panic of 1837.
    (1) Causes, immediate and remote.
    (2) Effects.
        a. Economic.
        b. Political.
    (3) Remedies and Van Buren's attitude.

The Campaign of 1840

1. Nature and significance.
2. Harrison-Tyler administration.

New Era of Intellectual and Material Development, 1820–1840

1. Old world awakening.
    (1) Great revolutions on the continent.
    (2) Reforms in England.
2. New intellectual life in America.
    (1) In literature, Hawthorne, Poe, Whittier, Longfellow, Bancroft, Emerson, Holmes, Prescott and Lowell.
    (2) In political and economic science, Kent, Story, Lieber and Carey.
    (3) Modern newspaper established.
    (4) Social reforms.
        a. New prison system.
        b. Increase of benevolent institutions.

(5) Political and moral reforms.

a. Rise of anti-slavery societies and their work.

b. Rise of great anti-slavery agitators.

c. Beginnings of a new political party.

3. New industrial conditions begin to appear.

(1) Steam navigation on rivers, lakes and ocean.

(2) Railways grow from 23 to over 2000 miles.

(3) Steam hammer and reaper invented.

(4) Corporations and labor organizations.

4. Significance of the new era.

(1) America rises in her own and in foreign estimation.

(2) Redistribution of population in the north.

(3) South remains comparatively stationary.

a. Causes.

b. Consequences.

References

Andrews, i. 363–390. Benton's Thirty Years' View, i. 220–265, 373–473, 556–568, 676–707. Von Holst's Constitutional and Political History, ii. 31–79, 172–218, 459–505. Niles' Weekly Register. (See index for topics in Vols. 33–66. Roosevelt's Thomas H. Benton, 114–156, 189–208. Schouler's History of the United States, iii. 469–475; iv. 44–54, 68–70, 168–174, 229–230, 257–272, 276–285. Schurz's Henry Clay, i. 351–355, 372–378; ii. 23–51, 113–127. Shepard's Martin Van Buren, 242–299. Sumner's Andrew Jackson as a Public Man, 224–276, 291–342. Woodrow Wilson's Division and Reunion, 69–98.

Conflict between Nationality and Slavery, 1820–1870

SECTIONALIZATION OF INTERESTS AND SENTIMENTS, 1835–1860

Nature of this Phase

1. State sovereignty becomes the instrument of slavery.
2. Disunion sentiment grows in both sections.
3. Rise of new parties in each section.

Slavery in Early Days

1. Not considered an evil in the 17th century.
   (1) Gained no solid foothold in the North.
   (2) Favored in South by climate, soil and products.
2. On the decline before the revolution.
   (1) Puritan and Quaker ideas not in harmony with it.
   (2) Even southern colonies petitioned against importation of slaves.
   (3) Attitude of England toward slavery in the colonies, 1660–1750.
   (4) Congress of 1774 declared against importation.
3. Effects of the revolution.
4. The contest in the constitutional convention.
5. Quaker petitions to the first congress and their effects.
6. First fugitive slave law—nature and effects.

Balance of Power between Freedom and Slavery in the Senate

1. Slavery loses control in the lower house; causes, particular and fundamental.
2. How power was maintained in the senate.
   (1) What was the order of state admission up to 1819, and what its meaning?
   (2) What was the meaning of Missouri's application in 1819?

Missouri Controversy and Compromise

1. Fundamental and immediate cause.
2. Talmadge's amendment or the Missouri limitation.
3. Leading arguments on each side.
4. Compare the spirit of slavery here with its spirit in the constitutional convention, and debates over the Quaker petitions.
5. The compromise and the effects of the fight. (Document XXXIX.)

References

Andrews', i. 340–347. Adams' John Randolph, 270–277. Benton's Thirty Years' View, i. 4–10, 14–18. Blaine's Twenty Years of Congress, i. 14–25, Draper's History of the American Civil War, i. 311–327, 349–359. Gilman's James Monroe, 144–149. Greeley *and* Cleveland *comp.*, Political Text-book for 1860, 49–65. Hart's Formation of the Union, 19–21, 107–109, 113–115, 126–127, 151–152, 170, 216, 236–241. Von Holst's Constitutional and Political History, i. 354–381. McLaughlin's Lewis Cass, 42–44. Nicolay *and* Hay's Abraham Lincoln: A History (*see* Century XXXIII (1887): 685–690. Roosevelt's Thomas H. Benton, 43–45.

Schouler's History of the United States, iii. 134–186. United States—Congress. Annals. Arnold's Lincoln and Slavery, 25–32. Greeley's American Conflict, i. 24–49. Wilson's Rise and Fall of the Slave Power, i. 1–56.

The Movement for Texas

1. Early attempts to possess Texas.
   (1) Relation to purchase of Louisiana.
   (2) Relation to purchase of Florida, 1819.
   (3) Mexican independence and its relation to this movement.
      a. Integrity of national domain a principle of action.
      b. Hence refused offers for Texas made in 1827, in 1829, and in 1835 including California.
   (4) Significance of offers to purchase Texas.
2. Another movement for Texas.
   (1) Slaveholders migrate to Texas.
      a. Purpose at first, perhaps only industrial.
      b. Effects.
   (2) General Huston, encouraged by President Jackson, inaugurates rebellion in Texas.
   (3) Calls for aid from United States.
   (4) Declaration of independence without the "equal rights of man", 1836.
   (5) Victory of San Jacinto won by men and munitions from United States, 1836.
   (6) Independence recognized.

2. Annexation of Texas.
   (1) Two obstacles.
      a. Danger from Mexico.
      b. Hostility of anti-slavery sentiment—causes and effects.
2. Attitude of parties and leaders, 1844.
   (1) Agreement between Van Buren and Clay.
   (2) Effect of this position on both.
   (3) Organization of Liberty party and its relation to the election.
   (4) Act of Annexation, 1845.

Mexican War

1. Causes.
   (1) Remote and fundamental causes.
   (2) Immediate and particular causes.
2. The war, 1846–1848.
   (1) Leading campaigns against Mexico proper.
      a. General Taylor's victories.
      b. General Scott captures the capital.
   (2) Conquest of California.
      a. Northern California occupied by American citizens.
      b. Fremont's expedition and its meaning.
   (3) Attitude of people and parties.
      a. Democratic party enthusiastic, specially in the South.
      b. Whig party opposed to war, except in the South, but supports war measures.

c. Anti-slavery party violently opposed.

d. People of all parties filled the army.

(4) Wilmot Proviso and its significance.

Campaign of 1848

1. Mexican war creates a Whig military hero, Gen. Taylor.
2. Produced none for administration party.
3. Clay and Webster put aside for Taylor. Reasons and significance.
4. General Cass nominated by the Democrats.
5. Free-soil party.
   (1) Successor to Liberty party.
   (2) Leading principles. (Document XL.)
   (3) Martin Van Buren its candidate.
      a. Motives of candidate and party.
      b. New York, the pivotal state, won by the Whigs.
      c. Free-soil vote; over 290,000 in the nation and over 120,000 in New York.

References

Andrews, ii. 3–29. Benton's Thirty Years' View, i. 665–676; ii. 94–97, 581–619, 639–649, 677–694, 722–724. Blaine's Twenty Years of Congress, i. 26–40, 62–86. Curtis' Life of Daniel Webster, i. 521–527; ii. 300–310, 332–342. Draper's History of American Civil War, i. 308–401. Greeley's American Conflict, i. 147–178, 185–198; *and* Cleveland *comp.* Political Text-Book of 1860, 15–18, 65–69. Von Holst's Constitutional and Political History, ii. 548–714; iii. 61–400. Lodge's Daniel Webster, 264–297. Roosevelt's Thomas H. Benton, 290–316. Schouler's History of the United States, iv. 247–257, 302–307, 518–545; v. 1–110. Schurz's Henry Clay, i. 162–165; ii. 270–314. Shepard's Martin

Van Buren, 306–308, 343–370. Sumner's Andrew Jackson, 351–359. Henry Wilson's History of the Rise and Fall of the Slave Power in America, i. 585–651; ii. 6–30, 114–160. Woodrow Wilson's Division and Reunion, 149–160.

The Compromise of 1850

1. Causes.
   (1) Remote and fundamental.
   (2) Immediate and particular.
2. Leading features of Clay's original propositions. (Document XLI.)
3. How propositions were received.
   (1) Opponents of the compromise.
      a. Congress opposed to plan as a whole.
      b. President Taylor. Reasons.
      c. Anti-slavery leaders.
      d. John C. Calhoun; his last great speech.
   (2) Supporters.
      a. Clay and Webster; their speeches.
      b. Men who feared disruption of union.
   (3) Agitation among people increases.
      a. South meets in convention in Nashville.
      b. Great excitement in New England over Webster's speech.
   (4) Main features passed after death of Taylor and Calhoun.
1. Immediate effects.
   (1) Excitement allayed and union meetings held.
   (2) Considered a "finality" by old parties.

(3) Deceptive calm; proof.

5. Fugitive slave law exasperates the North.
   (1) By its unusual provisions.
   (2) By its enforcement.

References

Andrews, ii. 30–37. Arnold's History of Lincoln and the Overthrow of Slavery. Blaine's Twenty Years of Congress, i. 76–108. Calhoun's Works, iv. 339–361, 542–574. Clay's Life and Speeches, iv. 595–602, 617–619, 593; vi. 394–418, 426–482, 515–568, 609. Draper's History of the American Civil War, i. 405. Greeley's American Conflict, i. 202–221; *and* Cleveland, *comp.* Political Text-Book of 1860, 69–79. Von Holst's Constitutional and Political History, iii. 402–597; iv. 1–45, 101–132. Johnston's History of American Politics, 151–157. Lalor's Cyclopedia of Political Science, *art.* Compromises (Alexander Johnston) i. 552–553; *art.* Fugitive Slave Laws (Alexander Johnston) ii. 315–317; *art.* Personal Liberty Laws (Johnston) iii. 162–163; *art.* Slavery (Johnston) iii. 735. Morse's Abraham Lincoln, i. 85–93. Nicolay *and* Hay's Abraham Lincoln: A History (*see* Century, XXXIII, 1887: 691–706). Roosevelt's Thomas H. Benton, 43–48, 157–171, 235–244, 332–339. Schouler's History of the United States, v. 133–157, 160–173, 178–187, 196–213. Woodrow Wilson's Division and Reunion, 161–193.

Campaign of 1852

1. Candidates and platforms of the old parties.
2. Free-soil party and principles.
3. Progress of the canvass.
   (1) Attitude of the northern and southern Whigs.
   (2) Many Free Soilers in 1848 now support Pierce.
4. The election—results and significance.

Kansas-Nebraska Bill, 1854

1. Nature and purpose.
2. Doctrine involved and its previous history.
3. Relation to compromises of 1850 and 1820.

Contest for Kansas Begins.

1. Missourians cross the border early.
2. Emigrant Aid Society.
   (1) Authorized by legislature of Massachusetts.
   (2) First colony departs July, 1854.
      a. Inspired the North.
      b. Hundreds of committees formed.
3. Slaveholders fail in establishing like organizations. Why?
4. Elections in Kansas.
5. Governors appointed and their experience.
6. Conflicting constitutions.
   (1) Attitude of administration.
   (2) Debates in congress.
   (3) Civil war in Kansas.
   (4) Kansas and the congressional bribe.
7. Political revolution.
   (1) Free-soil men with an old platform, a new candidate, and a new name.
   (2) Whigs and Know-nothings.
   (3) Disintegration of northern democracy and its significance.
   (4) Meaning of the vote.

References

Andrews, i. 38–56. Draper's History of the Civil War, i. 409–417. Greeley's American Conflict, i. 235–251, *and* Cleveland *comp.* Political Text-Book of 1860, 18–26. Von Holst's Constitutional and Political History, iv. 133–461 ; v. 1–468. Johnston's History of American Politics, 156–169. Morse's Abraham Lincoln, i. 93–110. Nicolay *and* Hay's Abraham Lincoln : A History (*see* Century xxxiii (1887) : 866–884, xxiv : 82–110). Roosevelt's Thomas H. Benton, 341–365. Schouler's History of the United States, v. 239–250, 280–308, 315–336, 342–363. Schurz's Henry Clay, ii. 373–405. Tourgée's Hot Plowshares. Henry Wilson's History of the Rise and Fall of the Slave Power in America, ii. 360–434, 462–522. Woodrow Wilson's Division and Reunion, 178–193.

Dred Scott Decision

1. The case ; its nature, purpose and decision.
2. Relation to Missouri compromise and Kansas trouble.
3. Political effects.
   (1) On state campaigns of 1858.
   (2) On Supreme Court.

Lincoln-Douglas Debate, 1858

1. Preliminary to the battle. (Document XLII.)
2. Position of Douglas and his qualifications for a hand-to-hand contest.
3. Position of Lincoln and his qualifications
4. The canvass. (Document XLIII.)
   (1) Seven joint debates and a number of single speeches.
   (2) Topics and methods of debate.
5. Results of contest.

(1) To the contestants.
(2) To their parties.

John Brown's Raid

1. Another preliminary skirmish.
2. Brown's antecedents.
3. His purpose, plans and their execution.
   (1) How far known by the North.
   (2) What the South believed.
4. Effect on the country.
5. Real significance of raid.

References

Andrews, ii. 57-65. Blaine's Twenty Years of Congress, i. 130–137, 154–158. Draper's History of American Civil War, i. 407–408, 525–530. Greeley's American Conflict, i. 279–299. Von Holst's Constitutional and Political History, vi. 1-37, 253–324; vii. 18–60. Lalor's Cyclopedia of Political Science, *art.* John Brown (Johnston) i. 310; *art.* Secession (Johnston) iii. 698. Morse's Abraham Lincoln, i. 111–160. Nicolay *and* Hay's Abraham Lincoln: A History. (*See* Century, xxxiv (1887): 203–219, 369–386, 516–524.) Nicolay *and* Hay's Abraham Lincoln: A History, ii. 58–170. Schouler's History of the United States, v. 376–382, 437–447. U. S.—Senate Reports, 1859–1860. Report of Com. No. 278. Henry Wilson's History of the Rise and Fall of Slave Power in America, ii. 523–533, 587–600. Woodrow Wilson's Division and Reunion, 197–199, 202–204.

Charleston Convention and Disruption of Democratic Party, 1860

1. Factions and their principles. (Doc. XLIV.)
2. Committee on platform and its reports.
3. Causes of the split, immediate and remote.
4. Subsequent conventions.
5. Significance of the breach.

Chicago Convention and the Nomination of Lincoln

1. Elements composing the convention.
2. Leading candidates.
3. Why Lincoln was nominated.
4. The platform, its ideas and their origin.

Constitutional Union Party

1. Component elements.
2. Leading ideas.
3. Candidates.

Canvass and the Election

1. General character.
   (1) Warm conflict of ideas and principles.
   (2) More intense in the North than in the South.
2. October elections.
   (1) Foretold triumph of Lincoln.
   (2) Patriotic conduct of Douglas.
3. An analysis of the vote; its meaning.

References

Abbott's History of the Civil War in America, i. 39–41. Arnold's History of Lincoln and the Overthrow of Slavery, 140–155. Blaine's Twenty Years of Congress, i. 154–178. Draper's History of the American Civil War, i. 496–507. Foote's War of the Rebellion, 264–294. Greeley's American Conflict, i. 309–318; Greeley *and* Cleveland, *camp.* Political Text-Book for 1860, 26–48. Von Holst's Constitutional and Political History, vii. 110–249. Johnston's History of American Politics, 179–180. Kettell's History of the Great Rebellion, i. 36–40. Lalor's Cyclopedia of Political Science, *art.* Democratic-Republican party (Johnston), i. 781–782. Lamon's Life of Abraham Lincoln, 424–440, 444–457.

Morse's Abraham Lincoln, i. 161–179. Nicolay *and* Hay's Abraham Lincoln: A History. (*See* Century xxxiv. (1887): 203–219, 369–386. Nicolay *and* Hay's Abraham Lincoln: A History, ii. 227–295. Schouler's History of the United States, v. 454–469. Victor's History of the Southern Rebellion, i. 31–35. Henry Wilson's History of the Rise and Fall of Slave Power in America, ii. 673–704. Woodrow Wilson's Division and Reunion, 204–210.

THE FINAL STRUGGLE BETWEEN NATIONALITY AND SLAVERY, 1860–1870

Nature of this Struggle

1. A measure of the strength of national sentiment.
2. A revival of nationality.

Movement for Secession

1. Causes and motives. (Document XLVI.)
   (1) Fundamental and secondary.
   (2) False or specio
2. Active campaign.
   (1) Conspiracy of southern office-holders. (Document XLV.)
      a. National; cabinet and congressional.
      b. State; governors and others.
   (2) Special session of southern legislatures.
      a. Called by proclamations.
      b. Voted to organize for state defense.
      c. Issued calls for secession convention.
   (3) First set of conventions, Dec. 20, 1860—Feb. 1, 1861.

a. Why not by popular vote?

b. Opposition to secession in various states.

c. The ordinance; nature and meaning.

(4) How popular sentiment was aroused.

3. The South's appeal to right of revolution.

(1) Read statement of this doctrine in the Declaration of Independence.

(2) Compare the South's list of abuses with those in the Declaration.

(3) What conclusions?

Formation of the Confederacy

1. Preliminary steps.

(1) Delegates authorized by secession conventions.

(2) Convention urged by conspirators at Washington.

3. Montgomery convention, Feb. 4, 1861.

(1) Provisional constitution.

(2) Election of president and vice-president.

(3) Military preparations.

a. Confederacy to control ports, arsenals, public establishments.

b. 100,000 volunteers and $15,000,000 voted.

(4) Commissioners to Washington and to slave states not yet seceded.

Conspiracy at Washington

1. Influence over President Buchanan.

(1) Seen in his message to congress.
(2) In refusal to protect United States property in rebel states.

2. Disorganization of departments.
3. Plan of southern congressmen.
4. Threatened seizure of Washington and Lincoln.
   (1) Purpose and plan.
   (2) Measures taken to prevent it.

Attempts to Conciliate the South Dec., 1860, to April, 1861

1. Border states lead. Reasons.
2. Crittenden compromise.
   (1) Origin and nature.
   (2) Attitude of northern and southern senators.
3. The Committee of Thirty-three.
   (1) Origin and membership.
   (2) Propositions.
   (3) Cause of failure.
4. The peace convention.
   (1) Origin and work.
   (2) Attitude of seceded states.
      a. Causes.
      b. Effects on North and South.
5. Congressional action in organizing new territories.
   (1) No limitation upon slavery whatever.
   (2) Significance of this action.
6. Attitude of the new administration.

(1) Seward's great change.
(2) Lincoln's inaugural. (Document XLVII.)
(3) Treatment of confederate commissioners.
7. The gain and loss in this policy.
(1) To the South.
(2) To the North.
a. With reference to free states.
b. With reference to border slave states.

Attack on Sumter

1. Immediate cause.
2. Effect on the South.
3. Effects on the North.

References

Andrews, ii. 75–104. Blaine, i. 215-274. Botts' Great Rebellion, 177–179, 183–226. Draper's History of the American Civil War, ii. 41–93. Greeley's American Conflict, i. 338-516. Harper's New Monthly Magazine, xxii : 111–112, 255–257, 404–406, 546–549, 688–691. Johnston's Representative American Orations, iii. 58–124, Logan's Great Conspiracy, 99–188, 255–275. Morse's Abraham Lincoln, i. 180–254. Nicolay *and* Hay's Abraham Lincoln, ii. 296–447 ; iii. 1–449 ; iv. 44–244; Works of Lincoln, ii. 1–34 ; (*see* Cent. xxxiv. (1887) : 819–850 ; xxxv. 64–87, 265–284, 419–436, 599–616, 707–723, 898–922.) Ropes' Story of the Civil War, i. 1–97. Henry Wilson's Rise and Fall of the Slave Power, iii. *see* table of contents. Woodrow Wilson's Division and Reunion, 210–221.

Leading Military Events up to 1863

1. The great military objects of the war.
(1) The capture of each other's capital.
(2) The possession of the Mississippi river.
(3) Control of the Atlantic ports.

2. General advantages and disadvantages to each party with reference to each of these objects.
3. Battle of Bull Run, July, 1861.
   (1) Previous engagements.
   (2) Immediate cause and its meaning.
   (3) Some features of the battle.
   (4) Results.
      a. Immediate and remote to each party.
      b. Judged by the ends in view.
4. Breaking the confederate lines in the West, Nov., 1861—Dec., 1862.
   (1) Location of first line and its means of defense.
   (2) Federal attack.
      a. Plan and means.
      b. Capture of Forts Henry and Donelson.
      c. Results.
   (3) Second line of defense.
      a. Location.
      b. Shiloh and the fall of Corinth.
      c. Other results.
   (4) Third line of defense.
      a. Vicksburg; its strong position.
      b. Grant drives Pemberton within his fortifications, Dec., 1862.
5. Campaign for capture of Richmond.
   (1) Double purpose.
      a. Protection of Washington.
      b. Capture of Richmond.

(2) Preparation.

(3) The Peninsula campaign, March, 1860—Aug., 1862.

a. Leading events.

b. Results of the movement as a whole.

6. Campaign against Washington, Aug.—Dec., 1862.

(1) Favorable conditions.

a. McClellan's retreat rouses the enthusiasm of the South.

b. Increase of confederate army by conscription.

c. Coöperating sortie in the West.

(2) Creation of army of Virginia with Pope in command.

(3) Second battle of Bull Run.

a. Lee's plan of attack.

b. Some features of the battle.

c. Why the federal troops were defeated.

d. Results.

(4) Lee invades Maryland and Bragg Kentucky. (Document XLVIII.)

a. What they hoped to accomplish.

b. Harper's Ferry and Antietam.

(5) Battle of Fredericksburg.

a. Circumstance leading to it.

b. Causes of federal defeat.

(6) Results of the campaign.

a. To the South.

b. To the North.

References

Andrews, ii. 105–153. Draper's History of the American Civil War, ii. 108–130, 258–326, 367–417, 427–479. Grant's Personal Memoirs, i. 282–421. Greeley's American Conflict, i. 531–654. Logan's Great Conspiracy, 276–341. Morse's Abraham Lincoln, i. 298–302, 303–367; ii. 1–94. Nicolay *and* Hay's Abraham Lincoln, iv. 308–340; v. 42–122, 148–200, 252–287, 303–440; vi. 1–29, 131–222; (*see* Cent xxxvi. (1888): 281–305, 393–402, 562–583, 658–678, 212–933; xxxvii.: 130–148, 427–439.) Rope's Story of the Civil War, i. 111–274. Sherman's Personal Memoirs, i. 204–291.

Foreign Relations and Naval Operations to 1863

1. Blockade of southern ports.
   (1) By president's proclamation, April 1861.
   (2) Political significance.
   (3) The South recognized as belligerents by England and France.
2. English sentiment. (Document XLIX.)
   (1) Against the North.
      a. Commercial reasons.
      b. Influence of slavery.
      c. Effect of Bull Run.
      d. Effect on the North.
   (2) Position of English government.
      a. Charged with favoring partition of the republic.
      b. Prime minister and Mr. Gladstone.
      c. Prince Albert and Queen Victoria.
   (3) Feeling by classes.

a. Upper and middle.
b. Laboring classes.
(4) Newspapers.
3. The Trent affair.
(1) The South hopes for European aid.
a. Agents early sent abroad.
b. Unofficially received by English government.
c. Appointment of Mason and Slidell.
(2) Capture of the Trent by the San Jacinto.
(3) Effects on England.
(4) Action of American authorities; effects.
4. England the naval base of the confederacy.
(1) Confederacy had but few home-made privateers.
a. Reasons.
b. Why it turned to England.
(2) English shipyards built five privateers besides ironclads and rams.
(3) The Alabama.
a. Her origin and work.
b. Capture by the Kearsarge, June, 1864.
c. America complained that the Alabama
Was made in England.
Had an English armament.
Was manned by Englishmen.
Had artillerists in English pay.
Sailed under English flag.

Was welcomed in English ports.
Never saw an American harbor.

d. English reply: "Can not change domestic laws to please foreign nations."

e. America's answer.

5. American navy.
   (1) Condition in 1861.
      a. 42 vessels, 555 guns and 7600 men.
   (2) Duties in the war.
6. Early naval engagements.
   (1) Merrimac and Monitor, March, 1862.
      a. Origin of each.
      b. First day's work at Hampton's Roads.
      c. Conflict and its results.
   (2) Capture of New Orleans, May, 1862.
      a. Importance of the place.
      b. Confederate fortifications and other obstacles.
      c. Federal forces and their preparation.
      d. Passing the forts.
      e. Surrender of the city.
      f. Farragut moves up to Vicksburg.

References

Blackwood's Edinburgh Magazine. *See* index 1861–1865 for British opinion. Boynton's History of the Navy during the Rebellion, i. 75–184, 358–376, 515–566. Draper's History of the American Civil War, ii. 27–33, 501–548. Gaspin's America Before Europe, 1–322. Greeley's American Conflict, i. 606–608 Harper's New Monthly Magazine xxiv.: 115, 258, 398–401, 550–551; xxv.; 418, 563; xxvi.: 131, 272, 412, 560–561. McCarthy's His-

tory of Our Own Times, iii. 233-278. Morse's Abraham Lincoln, iv. 266-280; v. 21-41, 218-274; vi. 49-89; viii. 254-280; ix. 128-157. Quarterly Review. *See* index 1861-1865 for British opinion.

Movement for Emancipation

1. Motives of the North in the war.
   (1) Preservation of the Union.
   (2) Destruction of slavery.
2. Northern concessions to prevent disunion.
   (1) Held many border state men.
   (2) Prevented early dissensions in the North.
3. Irregular action by military authorities.
   (1) General Butler declares slaves contraband, May, 1861.
      a. Circumstances.
      b. Significance.
   (2) General Fremont's action, August, 1861.
   (3) Secretary Cameron's action, 1861.
   (4) General Hunter's declaration, 1862.
   (5) Halleck, Buell, Hooker, and McClellan.
4. Anti-slavery legislation of congress.
   (1) Slaves used in the rebel army to be free, Aug., 1861.
      a. How and why used in war.
      b. Opposition to the bill and its meaning.
   (2) Army prohibited from returning slaves, March, 1862.
   (3) Abolition of slavery in District of Columbia, April, 1862.

(4) Prohibition of slavery in the territories, June, 1862.

(5) Employment of the colored soldiers, July, 1862.

a. Cause and nature of bill.

b Great indignation excited in the border states.

(6) Confiscation Act—its nature, July, 1862.

a. Opposition in North and in border states.

b. Possible effects.

5. President Lincoln's early anti-slavery acts.

(1) Lincoln's position as shown in his inaugural and his letters to Greeley and Bancroft.

(2) Colonization proposed; first annual message.

(3) Compensated emancipation proposed.

a. Intended for border states; reasons.

b. Attitude of these states; cause and effect.

6. Emancipation. (Document L.)

(1) Urged upon Lincoln early; why he waited.

(2) Lincoln begins to consider a preliminary proclamation.

(3) Proclamation, Sept. 23, 1862.

a. Immediate cause.

b. Nature and scope.

(4) Immediate effects.
   a. Action of governors and congressmen.
   b. "Divided the North and united the South."

(5) The final proclamation.
   a. Its nature.
   b. Effects on foreign nations.
   c. Effects on the South.
   d. Expectation of the negro.

References

Andrews, ii. 190–193. Arnold's History of Lincoln and the Overthrow of Slavery, 226–228, 233–237, 247–305. Blaine's Twenty Years of Congress, i. 342–343, 368–377, 345–348. Draper's History of the American Civil War, ii. 590–614. Greeley's American Conflict, ii. 237–265. Harper's New Monthly Magazine xxv.: 839; xxvi. 411–412. Logan's Great Conspiracy, 342–512. Morse's Abraham Lincoln, ii. 1–30, 96–133. Nicolay *and* Hay's Abraham Lincoln, iv. 385–396, 416–439; v. 201–217; 90–130, 147–172, 399–488; (*see* Cent. xxxvii. (1888–1889): 276–294, 440–447. 689–704, 917–922.) Works of Lincoln, ii. See topics in index. Henry Wilson's Rise of the Slave Power, ii. 230–393.

Politics During 1861 and 1862 (Document LI.)

1. Differentiation of sentiment among the people.

(1) Extreme anti-slavery men.
   a. Opposed to president's moderate policy.
   b. Number, leader and influence.

(2) Moderate Republicans and War Democrats.
   a. Constituted majority of northern people.
   b. Furnished majority of volunteers.

c. War Democrats furnished majority of army officers.

(3) Moderate Democrats.

a. Peculiar attitude toward the rebellion.

b. Sided with McClellan against Lincoln.

c. Afterward became "Peace" Democrats.

(4) Copperheads.

a. "Northern men with southern principles."

b. Where strongest; causes.

c. How they hindered the war.

d. Feeling toward them.

2. General issues of campaign of 1862.

(1) Really a choice between nationality and slavery.

a. Majority of people hardly conscious of this.

b. How it became the issue.

(2) How the opposition stated the issue.

a. An abolition war.

b. Administration deceiving the people.

3. Campaigns in various states.

(1) Northern border states.

(2) In the Empire state.

1. Election results.

(1) Immediate.

a. Republicans defeated in five great states.

b. New England reduces its majorities.

c. Border states save the administration and save the nation. Why they did.

d. Republican majority in house of representatives reduced to about 20.

(2) Indirect effects.

a. Emboldened opposition to the war.

b. Talk of foreign mediation.

References

Arnold's History of Lincoln and the Overthrow of Slavery, 214–230. Blaine's Twenty Years of Congress, i. 313–346, 415–445. Morse's Abraham Lincoln, ii. 95–133. Nicolay *and* Hay's Abraham Lincoln, iv. 64–108, 370–384; vii. 361–368.

The Year 1863

1. Depression of the North in spring of 1863.

(1) Extent and causes.

(2) Effects.

a. Growing desire for peace.

b. Increase of organized opposition.

2. Case of Vallandigham.

(1) His opposition in congress.

(2) Speech at Mt. Vernon, Ohio.

a. Occasion.

b. Nature and effects.

(3) Arrest, trial, and sentence.

(4) Agitation for his release. (Document LII.)

(5) Results.

a. Nominated for governor of Ohio.

b. Accepted leader of organized opposition to the war.

3. Draft of 1863.
   (1) Nature of the law.
   (2) Necessity for the draft.
   (3) Opposition.
4. New York riots, July 13, 1863.
   (1) Causes.
   (2) The riots and their effects.

Leading Military Events of 1863

1. Capture of Vicksburg.
   (1) Significance of the place.
   (2) Its defenses.
   (3) Some features of the attack and siege.
   (4) Surrender and its consequences.
2. Operations in vicinity of Charleston.
   (1) Leading military events.
   (2) Leading naval events.
3. Confederate sortie northward.
   (1) Causes.
   (2) Purpose of the campaign.
   (3) Condition and position of the two armies.
   (4) Movements northward.
   (5) Battle of Gettysburg.
      a. Some of its features.
      b. Why it was fought.
   (6) Results.
4. Army of the Cumberland.
   (1) Origin and relation to other armies.
   (2) Bragg's sortie into Kentucky in 1862.

(3) Battle of Chickamauga, Sept., 1863.
  a. Connecting movements.
  b. The battle and results.
(4) Reorganization of forces in the West.
(5) Siege of Chattanooga.
  a. Relative forces.
  b. Hooker's troops transferred from the Rapidan.
  c. Longstreet sent to relieve Knoxville.
  d. Arrival of Grant; supply routes opened.
  e. Sherman moves from Vicksburg to Chattanooga.
  f. Battle and its results, Nov., 1863.
(6) Sherman hastens to relieve Burnside at Knoxville.

References

Andrews, ii. 130–136. 154–157. Arnold's History of Lincoln and the Overthrow of Slavery, 398–433. Blaine's Twenty Years of Congress, i. 488–497. 509–512, Draper's History of the Civil War, iii. 25–103, 125–259. Greeley's American Conflict, ii. 286–322, 367–646, 484–511. Harper's New Monthly Magazine, xxvii: 273–274, 846–848. Morse's Abraham Lincoln, ii. 134–199. Nicolay *and* Hay's Abrahan Lincoln, vii. 1–57, 112–395; viii. 43–188; *see* Cent. xxxvii. (1888–1889): 917–932; xxxviii.; 123–148.)

The Financial Problem of the War

1. Condition of treasury at opening of war.
  (1) Deficit in 1861.
  (2) Results.
2. Early congressional expedients.
  (1) Small loans on short time.

(2) Why only pressing needs were met.

3. Morrill tariff.
   (1) Purpose and nature.
   (2) Effects.
4. Secretary Chase's report and action of congress.
   (1) Estimate for first fiscal year over $300,-000,000.
   (2) Means for more revenue.
   (3) Results.
      a. Opposition among taxpayers.
      b. Taxes were short $30,000,000 at end of first year.
      c. Loans reached nearly $200,000,000 by Dec., 1861.
5. Suspension of specie payment, 1861.
   (1) Immediate causes.
   (2) Results.
6. Establishment of a national currency.
   (1) Causes of the legal tender act.
   (2) Spaulding's bill, Dec., 1861.
      a. $150,000,000 of treasury notes.
      b. Legal tender, except for duties on imports and interest on the public debt.
      c. Notes changeable into bonds.
   (3) Arguments against the bill.
   (4) Arguments for the bill.
   (5) Results.
      a. Worked so well that larger issues were authorized.

b. Revival in trade.
c. Helped save elections of 1862.

7. Internal revenue system.
   (1) Insufficiency of legal tender act.
   (2) Preceding acts of internal taxation.
   (3) Act of July, 1862.
      a. Hardly anything escaped.
      b. Raised almost $1,000,000 each day.
      c. Put credit of the nation on a safe basis.

8. National finances and state banks.
   (1) Attitude of state banks.
   (2) How legal tender act hastened national banking system.
      a. Greenbacks had become popular.
      b. National taxes required in legal tender paper.
      c. Tax collectors personally responsible for money deposited with banks.
      d. Bonds seemed to furnish a secure basis for the system.

9. National banking system, Feb., 1863.
   (1) Introduced by Senator Sherman.
   (2) Leading points.
      a. Union notes of equal value.
      b. National bonds deposited for redemption of bank notes.
      c. Possible for state banks to become national banks.

(3) Opposition.
(4) Results of the system.

10. Cost of the war.
(1) Above were mostly modes of carrying debts.
(2) National debt.
(3) Debts of states.
(4) Other expenditures.
a. By organizations.
b. By individuals.
(5) Destruction of property.
a. Directly by war.
b. Indirectly by deranging trade and industry.
(6) Grand total indicates what patriotism was willing to pay for the Union.

References

Andrews, ii. 186–190. Blaine's Twenty Years of Congress, i. 396–487. Draper's History of the American Civil War, ii. 549–576; iii. 491–497. Nicolay *and* Hay's Abraham Lincoln, iii. 238–244; vi. 223–252; (*see* Cent. xxxvii. (1888–1889): 553–559.) Woodrow Wilson's Division and reunion, 229–221, 232–233.

The Political Campaign of 1864

1. Questions involved and the attitude of factions.
2. Republican opposition to president.
(1) Causes.
(2) Danger.
3. Chase's campaign for the nomination.
(1) Logical leader of the radical element. Proof.

(2) Congressional committee to promote his canvass.
(3) Why Chase withdrew.

4. Cleveland convention.
   (1) Origin and leaders.
   (2) Purpose.
   (3) The convention itself.
5. Renomination of Lincoln. (Document LIII.)
   (1) Attitude of the people and how made known.
   (2) Baltimore convention and its work, June, 1864.
6. Chicago convention, August 29, 1864.
   (1) Postponement of meeting and reasons.
   (2) Effects on the Republicans.
   (3) Platform. (Document LIII.)
   (4) Candidates and McClellan's acceptance.
   (5) Vallandigham criticizes the candidate.
7. The campaign and its partizan bitterness.
8. Result—immediate and remote.

References

Blaine's Twenty Years of Congress, i. 513-532. Draper's History of the American Civil War, iii. 470–479. Greeley's American Conflict, ii. 654-677. Morse's Abraham Lincoln, ii. 346–315. Nicolay *and* Hay's Abraham Lincoln, viii. 309–325; ix. 29-127, 244–262, 351–384; (*see* Cent. xxxviii. (1889); 278–298, 406–426, 546–551, 692–702.)

The Collapse of the Confederacy. (Document LIV.)

1. Lieutenant-General Grant and his work.
   (1) Position created by congress, Feb., 1864.

(2) Strength of armies.
(3) Leading events in Virginia and their results, May–March, 1865.
a. The Wilderness.
b. Spottsylvania.
c. The North Anna.
d. Cold Harbor.
e. Petersburg and Early's sortie.
f. Siege of Richmond.

2. Farragut in Mobile bay, Jan.–Aug., 1864.
(1) Defenses of the confederates.
(2) Farragut's fleet and flight.
(3) Results.

3. Sherman's campaigns, May, 1864–April, 1865.
(1) Capture of Atlanta.
a. Contributory events.
b. Significance.
(2) March to the sea ; purpose and effects.
(3) Hood's sortie.
a. Causes and purpose.
b. Battles of Franklin and Nashville.
c. Hood's disastrous retreat and its meaning.
(4) Sherman's return through the Carolinas.

4. Last movements, March–April, 1865.
(1) Purpose of Lee.
a. To evacuate Richmond.
b. To join General Johnston.

(3) Purpose of Grant.

(3) Leading events.

a. Battles around Richmond.

b. General assault on Lee's lines.

c. Evacuation of Richmond.

5. Appomattox.

(1) Terms of surrender and their significance.

(2) The surrender.

a. Some scenes and their significance.

b. Effects.

6. Johnston's surrender to Sherman.

(1) First meeting.

(2) Delay and arrangements repudiated by the authorities.

(3) Final arrangements.

7. Assassination of Lincoln and Grand Review.

References

Draper's History of the American Civil War, iii. 264–417, 521–634. Greeley's American Conflict, ii. 562–598, 625–684, 677–759. Nicholay *and* Hay's Abraham Lincoln, viii. 326–407; ix. 1–28, 158–183, 222–243, 263–331, 403–435, 464–496; x. 1–37, 148–302.

An Inside View of the Confederacy

1. Started with advantages.

(1) Organization completed before Lincoln's inaugural.

(2) Militia organized in 1860 and early in 1861.

(3) Early favorable impression on France and England.

2. Compelled to abandon state sovereignty.
3. Confederate congress a committee of public safety.
   (1) Held secret sessions; advantages and dangers.
   (2) Seized telegraph lines early in war.
   (3) Banished alien enemies and confiscated their property.
   (4) First conscription, April, 1862; significance.
   (5) Voted to sustain Davis' retaliatory measures.
   (6) Davis vetoed more bills of the provisional congress than all the presidents from Washington to Lincoln.
   (7) The "Debating Society on Capitol Hill".
4. Suppression of public opinion.
   (1) Slaveholders always resented criticism.
   (2) Anti-secession sentiment early suppressed.
   (3) Imprisonment without trial of suspected persons.
5. Financial depression.
   (1) Bonds at first in London sold before Union bonds.
   (2) Currency fell from $120 in 1861 to $6000 in 1865.
6. Military exhaustion and decay of military spirit.

(1) Conscription again, July, 1863, between 18 and 45.
(2) Davis appeals to women for aid in filling up ranks.
(3) Dec., 1863, another conscription, 18 to 55, under pain of desertion.
(4) Secretary of war reported from one-third to one-quarter of men absent.
(5) Dec., 1863, substitutes refused.
(6) Feb., 1865, all the men must serve in army or raise supplies.
(7) Again in 1865 all men between 17 and 55 liable to service.
(8) 60,000 Virginians were deserters.
(9) Driven to propose arming negroes; significance.

7. Condition of the armies at surrender.
8. Who deceived the people of the South.
   (1) Work of the clergy.
   (2) Davis and the politicians.
   (3) Work and responsibility of the press.

References

Draper's Civil War in America, iii. 479–490. Nicolay *and* Hay's Abraham Lincoln, x. 148–157. Pollard's Lost Cause, ch. 42.

The Reconstruction of the South

1. The constitutional question.
   (1) What is the real nature of the American union?

(2) Attitude of men and parties.

2. Creation of West Virginia.
   (1) Ancient feud between the parts of the Old Dominion.
   (2) Circumstances attending the split.
   (3) Admission of West Virginia; significance.
3. Lincoln's ideas of reconstruction.
   (1) "The union of these states is perpetual, hence
      a. No state . . can lawfully get out of the Union."
      b. The rights of the citizens of states in rebellion were not revoked but only interfered with.
      c. When the insurrection ceases, all loyal citizens resume their former rights and privileges.
   (2) Military governors.
   (3) Proclamation of amnesty, Dec., 1863.
4. Opposition to the president's plan.
   (2) Causes, fundamental and particular.
   (2) Bill passed by congress, July, 1864.
   (3) The pocket veto; reasons and effects.
5. 13th amendment.
   (1) Nature and necessity.
   (2) Opposition and defeat, June, 1864.
   (3) An issue in the presidential campaign.
   (4) Reintroduction and passage by aid of Democratic votes.

(5) Scenes in congress and at the White House.

6. President Johnson's work during the recess of congress.
   (1) Principle of his policy.
   (2) Work during summer and fall of 1865.
      a. An amnesty proclamation.
      b. Appointed provisional governors.
      c. Senators and representatives elected.

7. Legislation of the reconstructed states.
   (1) Laws affecting the negroes.
      a. Labor contracts.
      b. Vagrancy.
      c. Apprentice system for minors.
      d. Written contracts or the license system.
   (3) Causes and effects.

8. Breach between congress and the president.
   (1) Causes.
   (2) Congressional retaliation.

9. Congressional reconstruction.
   (1) 14th amendment.
   (2) Tenure of Office Act, and act to augment Grant's authority.
   (3) Great Reconstruction Act, March, 1867.
   (4) 15th amendment; nature, purpose and effects, 1870.
   (5) Freedmen's bureau.
      a. Origin and nature.
      b. Work and its effects.

10. Effects of congressional reconstruction.
    (1) Impeachment of President Johnson.
    (2) "Carpet-baggers". (Document LV.)
    (3) Kuklux Klan. (Document LV.)
    (4) Conflicts between national and state authorities.
    (5) Unsolved problems.

References

Barnes' History of the 39th Congress. Johnston's Representative Orations, 249–323. Letters relating to the Klux Klan iii. (*see* U. S.—House. 40th cong. 3d sess. Misc. doc. i. No. 23). Morse's Abraham Lincoln, ii. 216–245, 316–328. Nicolay *and* Hay's Abraham Lincoln. Woodrow Wilson's Division and Reunion, 254–272.

General Suggestions for Study

1. Purpose of these documents.

(1) To make clear to the student the continuity in the growth of American political ideas.

(2) To show what ideas dominated and characterized the various periods or phases of our political history.

(3) To impress the student that history presents problems for solution, and that these may be stated and solved with a greater degree of certainty than is generally believed.

(4) To create a desire to know history at first hand.

2. How to use the documents.

(1) Both the events indicated in the outline and the documents in this collection are means and not ends. They furnish the key to the life of the American people. They yield their results most readily and most richly when studied together. They should not be divorced; but each made to contribute to the understanding of the other.

(2) The questions and suggestions attached to the documents do not exhaust the possibilities, but are mainly aimed to lead the student into the heart of the document's meaning at once. They are not intended to lead to a study of the document

as a document, but to study the history in the document—get its content.

(3) The teacher must see that the student keeps up a constant comparison and contrast between the ideas presented in the various documents. The differences discovered will mark the progress in the growth of political ideas, while the resemblances will show the continuity of growth.

(4) Mastery of ideas and not of language should be the rule. In a few instances the student may be encouraged to learn the phraseology of portions of a document.

3. Where other original matter may be found.

(1) In government publications from the American Archives down to the Congressional Record.

(2) In the historical collections of various State Historical Societies.

(3) In the works of various notable men.

(4) The Old South Leaflets, of which the following are ready :

No. **1.** The Constitution of the United States. **2.** The Articles of Confederation. **3.** The Declaration of Independence. **4.** Washington's Farewell Address. **5.** Magna Charta. **6.** Vane's "Healing Question." **7.** Charter of Massachusetts Bay, 1629. **8.** Fundamental Orders of Connecticut, 1638. **9.** Franklin's Plan of Union, 1754. **10.** Washington's Inaugurals. **11.** Lincoln's Inaugurals and Emancipation Proclamation. **12.** The Federalist, Nos. 1 and 2. **13.** The Ordinance of 1787. **14.** The Constitution of Ohio.[1] **15.** Washington's Circular

[1] Double number, price 10 cents.

Letter to the Governors of the States, 1783. **16.** Washington's Letter to Benjamin Harrison, 1784. **17.** Verrazzano's Voyage. **18.** The Swiss Constitution.[1] **19.** The Bill of Rights, 1689. **20.** Coronado's Letter to Mendoza, 1540. **21.** Eliot's Narrative, 1670. **22.** Wheelock's Narrative, 1762. **23.** The Petition of Right, 1628. **24.** The Grand Remonstrance, 1641. **25.** The Scottish National Covenant, 1638. **26.** The Agreement of the People, 1648–9. **27.** The Instrument of Government, 1653. **28.** Cromwell's First Speech, 1653. **29.** The Discovery of America, from the Life of Columbus by his Son, Ferdinand Columbus. **30.** Strabo's Introduction to Geography. **31.** The Voyages to Vinland, from the Saga of Eric the Red. **32.** Marco Polo's Account of Japan and Java. **33.** Columbus's Letter to Gabriel Sanchez, describing the First Voyage and Discovery. **34.** Amerigo Vespucci's Account of his First Voyage. **35.** Cortes's Account of the City of Mexico. **36.** The Death of De Soto, from the "Narrative of a Gentleman of Elvas." **37.** Early Notices of the Voyages of the Cabots. **38.** Henry Lee's Funeral Oration on Washington. **39.** De Vaca's Account of his Journey to New Mexico, 1535. **40.** Manasseh Cutler's Description of Ohio, 1787. **41.** Washington's Journal of his Tour to the Ohio, 1770. **42.** Garfield's Address on the North-west Territory and the Western Reserve. **43.** George Rogers Clark's Account of the Capture of Vincennes, 1779. **44.** Jefferson's Life of Captain Meriwether Lewis. **45.** Fremont's Account of his Ascent of Fremont's Peak. **46.** Father Marquette at Chicago, 1673. **47.** Washington's Account of the Army at Cambridge, 1775. **48.** Bradford's Memoir of Elder Brewster. **49.** Bradford's First Dialogue. **50.** Winthrop's "Conclusions for the Plantation in New England." **51.** "New England's First Fruits," 1643. **52.** John Eliot's "Indian Grammar Begun." **53.** John Cotton's "God's Promise to his Plantation." **54.** Letters of Roger Williams to Winthrop. **55.** Thomas Hooker's "Way of the Churches of New England." (*Address Directors, Old South Meeting House, Boston.*)

[1] Double number, price 10 cents.

(5) American History Leaflets, of which the following are ready:

1.—The Letter of Columbus to Santangel announcing his Discovery.
2.—The Ostend Manifesto. 1854.
3.—Extracts from the Sagas describing the Voyages to Vinland.
4.—Extracts from Official Declarations of the United States embodying the Monroe Doctrine. 1789–1891. [Double number.
5.—Extracts from the Treaty of Paris of 1763, with the King's Proclamation.
6.—Extracts from papers relating to the Bering Sea Controversy. 1824–1891.
7.—Articles and Ordinances of the Confederation of New England. 1643–1684.
8.—Exact Text of the Constitution of the United States. 1787–1870.
9.—Papers relating to the Voyages of John Cabot. 1497–1498.
10.—Gov. McDuffie's Message on the Slavery Question. 1835.
11.—Jefferson's Proposed Instructions to the Virginia Delegation. 1774. [Double number.
12.—Ordinances and other Papers relating to Secession. 1860–1861.
13.—Coronado's Journey to New Mexico and the Great Plains. 1540–42.
14.—The Virginia and Kentucky Resolutions. 1798–99.
15.—Documents illustrating the Territorial Development of the United States.
16.—Appeal of the Independent Democrats. 1854.
17.—Plans of Union. 1690–1776.
18.—President Lincoln's Inaugurals. 1861–1865.
19.—Extracts from the Navigation Laws. 1646–1700
20.—Articles of Confederation and Preliminary Documents. 1776–1781.

21.—Documents relative to the Stamp Act. 1765–1766.

22.—Documents illustrating State Land Claims and Cessions. 1776–1802.

23.—Extracts from the Dred-Scott Decision. 1857.

24.—Documents relative to the Bank Controversy. 1829–1833.

Address, Lovell & Co., New York.

Colonial Documents

I.

TREATY BETWEEN VIRGINIA AND THE COMMONWEALTH

(American Archives, Fourth Series, Vol. I, p. 339.)

"1st. The Plantation of *Virginia*, and all the inhabitants thereof, shall be and remain in due subjection to the Commonwealth of *England*; not as a conquered country, but as a country submitting by their own voluntary act: and shall enjoy such freedoms and privileges as belong to the free people of *England*.

"2d. The General Assembly, as formerly, shall convene and transact the affairs of the colony.

"3d. The people of *Virginia* shall have a free trade, as the people of *England*, to all places, and all nations.

"4th. *Virginia* shall be free from all taxes, customs, and impositions whatsoever, and none shall be imposed on them, without the consent of their General Assembly; and that neither forts nor castles shall be erected, nor garrisons maintained, without their consent.

Suggestions for Study.

1 The position of Virginia in relation to England, and of Virginians as compared with Englishmen. Significance.

2 What is the general and particular meaning of sections 2 and 3?

3 Does section 4 indicate gain or loss? Prove.

II.

BACON'S DECLARATION IN THE NAME OF THE PEOPLE (1676)

(Massachusetts Historical Collections, Fourth Series, Vol. IX. p. 184.)

For having upon specious pretenses of public works raised great unjust taxes upon the commonalty for the advancement of private favorites and other sinister ends, but no visible effects in any measure adequate. For not having during this long time of his government . . . advanced this hopeful colony either by fortifications, towns or trade.

For having abused and rendered contemptible the magistrates of justice by advancing to places of judicature, scandalous and ignorant favorites.

For having wronged his majesty's pregorative

and interest by assuming a monopoly of the beaver trade.

For having protected and emboldened the Indians against his majesty's loyal subjects.

For having, when the army of the English was just upon the track of those Indians . . . sent back our army. . . .

For having with only the privacy of some few favorites, without acquainting the people, . . . forged a commission . . . for the raising and effecting civil war. . . .

Of this and the aforesaid we accuse Sir William Berkeley as guilty of every one of the same. . .

NATH. BACON,
General by consent of the People.

Topics for Study.

1 Make a list of the offenses charged against Berkley.

2 What relation did these bear to Bacon's rebellion ?

3 What is implied in the attitude of Bacon and his men ?

III.

EXTRACTS FROM THE BODY OF LIBERTIES, 1641

(Massachusetts Historical Collections, Fourth Series, Vol. VIII, p. 216–237.)

No man's life shall be taken away, no man's honor or good name shall be stained, no man shall be arrested, restrained, banished, dismembered . . . no man's goods or estate shall be taken away from him . . . unless it be by virtue or equity of some express law . . . established by a general court and sufficiently published, or in case of the defect of a law in any particular case by the word of God. . .

Every person within this jurisdiction, whether inhabitant or foreignor, shall enjoy the same justice and law . . . which we constitute and execute one toward another without partiality or delay. . . .

No monopolies shall be granted . . . but of such new institutions that are profitable to the country, and that for a short time. . . .

Every man whether inhabitant or foreigner, free or not free, shall have liberty to come to any public court, council or town meeting, and either by speech or writing to move any lawful . . . question or to present any necessary motion . . . or information.

Every man of or within this jurisdiction shall have free liberty, notwithstanding any civil power, to remove both himself, and his family . . . out of the same. . . .

No man's person shall be restrained or imprisoned by any authority whatsoever, before the law hath sentenced him thereto, if he can put in sufficient security . . . unless it be in crimes capital and contempts in open court. . . .

In all actions at law it shall be the liberty of the plaintiff and defendent by mutual consent to choose whether they will be tried by the bench or jury. . . . It shall be in the liberty of both . . . to challenge any of the jurors.

No man's person shall be arrested or imprisoned . . . for any debt or fine, if the law can find . . . satisfaction from his estate.

No man shall be twice sentenced by civil justice for one and the same crime, offence or trespass.

All jurors shall be chosen continually by the freemen of the town where they dwell.

Civil authority hath power . . . to deal with any church member in a way of civil justice, notwithstanding any church relation, office or interest.

No church censure shall degrade or depose any man from any civil dignity, office, or authority he shall have in the commonwealth.

Freemen of every township shall have power to make such laws and constructions as may concern the welfare of their town, provided that they be not of a criminal . . . nature . . . and that they be not repugnant to the public laws and orders of the country.

It is the constant liberty of the freemen of this plantation to choose yearly at the court of election all the general officers of this jurisdiction. . . . It is the liberty of the freemen to choose such deputies for the general court out of themselves, either in their own towns or elsewhere as they judge fittest.

If any man at his death shall not leave his wife a competent portion of his estate, upon just complaint made to the general court she shall be relieved.

When parents die intestate, the elder son shall have a double portion of his whole estate . . . unless the general court . . . shall judge otherwise.

All people of God within the jurisdiction who are not in a church way, and be orthodox in judgment, and not scandalous in life, shall have full liberty to gather themselves into a church estate.

Topics for Study.

1. Make a classification of the subjects included in above extracts.

2. Which of the above extracts embody ideas now operating in our government?

3. What ideas above are not found in our system of government? Inferences.

IV.

SAMUEL SHATTOCK'S LETTER (1661)

(Massachusetts Historical Collection, Fourth Series, Vol. IX, pp. 160-162,

. . . When we came into Boston harbor many came on ship-board for news and letters; but were struck in amaze when they saw what we were. . . . So I continued on ship-board . . . Expecting we might be sent for and finding otherwise, the master and myself fitted ourselves to go on shore to deliver our letter[1] to the governor. . . . The moderate sort . . . rejoiced to see me and some of the violent we met as men chained and bowed down, and could not look us in the face . . . we passed to the governor . . . ; so he required our hats to be pulled off, . . . had a few words to us, only asked me why I came again and why I did not send for my family. . . . We went on shore and were at a meeting. . . . On the morrow I passed to Salem

[1] Letter of Chas. II. commanding further proceeding against Quakers to cease.

where I was received with much joy and gladness of heart by many of the people of the town. And many friends did accompany me . . . to my dwelling where I found things all well. . . . And though cruelty hath greatly abounded, yet truth hath here gotten pretty much ground of the adversary ; and the coming of our ship is of wonderful service, for the bowels of the moderate sort are greatly refreshed, . . . and many mouths are now open . . . and some say it's the welcomest ship that ever came into this land. . . .

Topics for Study.

1. What light does this letter throw on the Quaker controversy in Massachusetts ?
2. What change in feeling toward the Quakers has taken place ? What is the significance of this ?
3. Why should Shattock take such pains to state just how he was received ?

V.

COMMERCE OF THE COLONIES IN 1750

(From Sheldon's American History.)

In the Southern Colonies.—(Charleston, S. C.) . . . They have a considerable trade both to Europe and the West Indies, whereby they become rich. . . . The merchants of Carolina are fair, frank traders. The gentlemen seated in the country are very courteous, live very noble in their houses, and give very genteel entertainment to all strangers and others that come to visit them.

The trade of Virginia . . . is . . . extensive. Tobacco is the principal article of it. . . . They ship also for the Madeiras, the Straihts (Gibraltar) and the West Indies, . . . grain, pork, lumber and cider; to Great Britain, bar-iron; . . . They think it a hardship not to have an unlimited trade to every part of the world.

In the Middle Colonies.——The trade of Pennsylvania is surprisingly extensive, carried on to Great Britain, the Madeiras, Lisbon, Cadiz, Holland, Africa, and the Spanish Main; . . . Their exports are provisions of all kinds, lumber, hemp, flax, iron, furs, and deerskins. . . . The Germantown thread stockings are in high estimation; the Irish settlers make very good linens, there are several other manufactures, (such as) of beaver hats, . . . superior in goodness to any in Europe.

The Pennsylvanians . . . are great republicans, and have fallen into the same errors in their ideas of independency as most of the other colonies. . . . However they are quiet, and concern themselves but little, except about getting money. . . .

New York. . . . They export chiefly grain, flour, pork, skins, furs, pig-iron, lumber and staves. . . . They also, as well as the Pennsylvanians, had erected several slitting mills to make nails, etc. But this is now prohibited (by parliament and they are exceedingly dissatisfied at it.)

The inhabitants . . . have a considerable trade with the Indians, for beavers, otter, raccoon skins, with other furs, and are supplied with venison and food in the winter and fish in the summer by the Indians, which they buy at an easy rate. . . .

In New England——In Rhode Island . . . they trade to Great Britain, Holland, Africa, the West Indies, and the neighboring colonies ; from Great Britain, (they import) dry goods ; from Holland, money; from Africa, slaves; from the West Indies, sugar, coffee and molasses; and from the neighboring colonies, lumber and provisions, and with what they purchase in one place they . . . (pay) in another. Thus, with the money they get in Holland, they pay their merchants in London; the sugars they get in the West Indies, they carry to Holland; the slaves they fetch from Africa they send to the West Indies, together with lumber and provisions; the rum that they distil they export to Africa; and with the dry goods which they purchase in London they traffic in the neighboring colonies. By this kind of circular commerce they subsist and grow rich.

(Those of Massachusetts) carry on a considerable traffic, chiefly in the manner of the Rhode Islanders, (exporting) salt fish and vessels. Of the latter they build annually a great number and send them, laden with cargoes of the former, to Great Britain, where they sell them.

VI.

RESTRICTIONS UPON COLONIAL COMMERCE

(Navigation Act of 1660.)

For the increase of shipping and the encouragement of the navigation of this nation, . . . be it enacted by the king's most excellent majesty and by the Lords and Commons . . . that . . . no goods or commodities whatsoever shall be imported into or exported out of any lands . . . to his majesty belonging . . . in any other ship . . . or vessels whatsoever, but in such ships or vessels as do truly . . . belong only to the people of England . . . or are built of, and belonging to any of the said lands . . . as the proprietors . . . and whereof the master and three-fourths of the mariners at least are English under the penalty of the forfeiture and loss of all the goods and commodities. (American History Leaflets, No. 19.)

(The Third Navigation Act 1672.)

. . . Be it enacted by the king's most excellent majesty . . . that . . . if any ship or vessel which by law may trade in any of your majesty's plantations shall come to any of them to ship and take on board any of the aforesaid commodities and . . . bond shall not be first given . . . to bring the same to England . . . and to no other place and there to unload and put the same on shore, . . . there shall be . . . paid to your majesty . . . so much of said commodities (according to) these following rates. . . .

Sugar, white, 112 lbs., five shillings.
Brown sugar, 112 lbs., one shilling and sixpence.
Tobacco, the pound, one penny.
Cotton-wool, the pound, one half-penny.
Indigo, the pound, twopence.
Ginger, 112 lbs., one shilling.
Logwood, 112 lbs., five pounds.
All other dyeing wood, the 112 lbs., sixpence.

. . . to be levied collected and paid to such collectors . . . as shall be appointed in the respective plantation . . . before the landing thereof . . . (American History Leaflets, No. 19.)

(The Act of 1699.)

Forasmuch as wool and woolen manufactures of cloth. . . are the greatest and most profitable commodities of this kingdom, on which the . . . trade of the nation do (es) chiefly depend, and whereas great quantities of the like manufactures have of late been made . . . in the English plantations in America and are exported from thence to foreign markets, heretofore supplied from England, which will . . . tend to the ruin of the woolen manufacture of this realm. . . . (Therefore) be it enacted by the king's most excellent majesty . . . that . . . no wool, woolen yarn, cloth, . . . or woolen manufactures whatsoever of any of the English plantations of America shall be laden . . . in any ship upon any pretence whatsoever ; as likewise that no such wool shall be laden upon horse, cart, or other carriage . . . to be exported . . . out of the said English plantations to any of the other of the said plantations or to any place whatsoever. (From Sheldon's American History.)

(The Act of 1732.)

Whereas, the art and mystery of making hats in Great Britain hath arrived to great perfection, and . . . his majesty's plantations in America have been wholly supplied with hats from Great Britain ; and whereas great quantities of hats have of late years been made . . . in America . . . wherefore, for preventing the said ill practices for the future, and for promoting . . . the trade of making hats in Great Britain, be it enacted . . . that . . . no hats (shall hereafter be made in America). (From Sheldon's American History.)

Documents on Period of the Revolution

VII.

JAMES OTIS ON THE WRITS OF ASSISTANCE

(From Tudor's Otis.)

I was desired by one of the court to look into the books, and consider the question now before them concerning the writs of assistance. And I take this opportunity to declare, that, whether under fee or not, I will to my dying day oppose with all the powers and faculties God has given me, all such instruments of slavery on the one hand, and villainy on the other, as this writ of assistance is.

It appears to me the worst instrument of arbitrary power, the most destructive of English liberty and the fundamental principles of law, that was ever found in an English law book.

I was solicited to argue this cause as Advocate-general; and because I would not, I have been charged with desertion from my office. I renounced that office, and I argue this cause from the same principle; and I argue it with the greater pleasure, as it is in favor of English liberty; . . . and it is in opposition to a kind of power, the exercise of which. . . . cost one king of England his head and another his throne.

Our ancestors as British subjects, and we, their descendants, as British subjects, were entitled to all those rights by the British constitution, as well as by the law of nature, and our provincial charters, as much as any inhabitant of London or Bristol, or any part of England; and were not to be cheated out of them by any phantom of 'virtual representation,' or any other fiction of law or politics.

Your honors will find in the old books concerning the office of a justice of the peace precedents of general warrants to search suspected houses. But, in more modern books, you will find only special warrants to search such and such houses, specially named, in which the complainant has before sworn that he suspects his goods are concealed; and will find it adjudged that special warrants only are legal . . . I rely on it that the writ being prayed for in this petition, being general, is illegal. It is a power that places the the liberty of every man in the hands of every petty officer.

But I deny that the writ now prayed for can be granted. . . . In the first place, the writ is universal, being directed to all 'and singular justices, sheriffs, constables, and all other officers and subjects;' so that in short it is directed to every subject in the king's dominions. Every one with this writ may be a tyrant in a legal manner, also may control, imprison, or murder any one within the realm. In the next place it is perpetual; there is no return. A man is accountable to no person for his doings. . . . In the third place, a person with this writ in the daytime may enter all houses, shops, etc. at will and command all to assist him. Fourthly, by this writ not only deputies, etc. but even their menial servants, are allowed to lord it over us. . . . Now, one of the most essential branches of English liberty is the freedom of one's house. A man's house is his castle; and whilst he is quiet is as well guarded as a prince in his castle. This writ . . . would totally annihilate this privilege. Custom-house officers may enter our houses when they please; we are commanded to permit their entry. Their menial servants may enter, may break locks, bars, and everything in their way; and whether they break through malice or revenge, no man, no court can inquire. Bare suspicion without oath is sufficient.

I will mention some facts. Mr. Pew had one of these writs, and, when Mr. Ware succeeded him, he indorsed this writ over to Mr. Ware; so that these writs are negotiable from one officer to another. Another instance is this: Mr. Justice Walley had called this same Mr. Ware before him by a constable to answer for breach of the Sabbath day. . . . As soon as he had finished, Mr.

Ware asked him if he had done. He replied, 'Yes.' 'Well then,' said Mr. Ware, 'I will show you a little of my power. I command you to permit me to search your house for uncustomed goods;' and went on to search the house from the garret to the cellar, and he served the constable in the same manner.

But to show another absurdity of this writ, I insist upon it that every person by the 14th of Charles the Second, has this power as well as the custom-houses officers. The words are, "It shall be lawful for any person," etc. What a scene does this open! Every man prompted by revenge, ill humor, or wantonness, to inspect the inside of his neighbor's house, may get a writ of assistance. Others will ask for it from self-defense; one arbitrary exertion will provoke another, until society be involved in tumult and blood.

(The court pronounced the following opinion. "The court has considered the subject of writs of assistance, and can see no foundation for such a writ, but as the practice in England is not known, it has been thought best to continue the question to the next term.")

(Of this speech John Adams said: "I do say in the most solemn manner that Mr. Otis's oration against writs of assistance breathed into this nation the breath of life.")

Topics for Papers.

Guard against making inferences that are not warranted by the facts given. This applies to the study of any document.

1 State the arguments given.

2 Do they prove the writs unconstitutional?

3 What right was guarded by a special writ that the general writ violated?

4 Did Otis prove or simply assert that Americans were entitled to all the rights of British subjects?

5 What is the "key-note" of this speech?

VIII.

PATRICK HENRY'S RESOLUTIONS (1765)

(Frothingham's Republic, 180.)

Whereas the honorable house of commons, in England, have of late drawn into question how far the general assembly of this colony hath power to enact laws for laying of taxes and imposing duties, payable by the people of this his majesty's most ancient colony: for settling and ascertaining the same to all future times, the house of burgesses of this present general assembly have come to the following resolves:—

Resolved, That the first adventurers, settlers of this His Majesty's colony and dominions of

Virginia, brought with them and transmitted to their posterity, and all other His Majesty's subjects since inhabiting in this His Majesty's colony, all the privileges and immunities that have at any time been held, enjoyed, and possessed by the people of Great Britain.

Resolved, That by two royal charters, granted by King James the First, the colony aforesaid are declared and entitled to all privileges and immunities of natural-born subjects, to all intents and purposes as if they had been abiding and born within the realm of England.

Resolved, That His Majesty's liege people of this his ancient colony have enjoyed the right of being thus governed by their own assembly in the article of taxes and internal police, and that the same have never been forfeited, or any other way yielded up, but have been constantly recognized by the king and people of Britain.

Resolved, therefore, That the general assembly of this colony, together with His Majesty or his substitutes, have, in their representative capacity, the only exclusive right and power to lay taxes and imposts upon the inhabitants of this colony ; and that every attempt to vest such power in any other person or persons whatever than the general assembly aforesaid, is illegal, unconstitutional and unjust, and have a manifest tendency to destroy British as well as American liberty.

Resolved, That His Majesty's liege people, the inhabitants of this colony, are not bound to yield obedience to any law or ordinance whatever, designed to impose any taxation whatsoever upon them, other than the laws or ordinances of the general assembly aforesaid.

Resolved, That any person who shall, by speaking or writing, assert or maintain that any person or persons other than the general assembly of this colony have any right or power to impose or lay any taxation on the people here, shall be deemed an enemy to His Majesty's colony.

Topics for Papers.

1 Search out the rights of Virginia asserted.

2 Do these rights belong to Virginia alone? Proof.

3 State on what grounds Virginia claims these rights?

4 Find the points of resemblance and difference between these resolutions and the speech of Otis.

IX.

DECLARATION OF RIGHTS BY CONGRESS OF 1765

The members of this congress, sincerely devoted, with the warmest sentiments of affection and duty, to His Majesty's person and government, inviolably attached to the present happy establishment of the protestant succession, and with minds deeply impressed by a sense of the present and impending misfortunes of the British colonies on this continent ; having considered as maturely as time will permit, the circumstances of the said colonies, esteem it our indispensable duty to make the following declarations of our humble opinion respecting the most essential rights and liberties of the colonists :

1 That His Majesty's subjects in these colonies owe the same allegiance to the crown of Great Britain that is owing from his subjects born within the realm, and all due subordination to that august body, the parliament of Great Britain.

2 That His Majesty's liege subjects in these colonies are entitled to all the inherent rights and liberties of his natural born subjects within the kingdom of Great Britain.

3 That it is inseparably essential to the freedom of a people, and the undoubted rights of Englishmen, that no taxes should be imposed on them, but with their own consent given personally, or by their representatives.

4 That the people of these colonies are not, and from their local circumstances, cannot be represented in the house of commons in Great Britain.

5 That the only representatives of the people

of these colonies are persons chosen therein by themselves; and that no taxes ever have been or can be constitutionally imposed on them, but by their respective legislatures.

6 That all supplies to the crown, being the free gifts of the people, it is unreasonable and inconsistent with the principles and spirit of the British constitution for the people of Great Britain to grant His Majesty the property of the colonists.

7 That trial by jury is the inherent and invaluable right of every British subject in these colonies. . . .

8 That it is the right of the British subjects in these colonies to petition the king or either house of parliament. . . .

Topics for Papers.

1 How many and what rights asserted?

2 What reasons given for claiming these?

3 What relations do the people of the colonies hold to king and parliament?

4 How then can they claim the rights above named?

5 How did Englishmen look upon a tax? See number 6.

6 Discover the resemblances with the two preceding documents, and draw conclusions.

X.

THE REPEAL OF THE STAMP ACT, 1766

(From Parliamentary History.)

Minister Granville said : " When I proposed to tax America, I asked the house if any gentleman would object to the right ; I repeatedly asked it, and no man would attempt to deny it. And tell me, when the Americans were emancipated ? When they want the protection of this kingdom, they are always very ready to ask it. That protection has always been afforded them in the fullest manner; and now they refuse to contribute their mite toward the public expenses. For let no gentlemen deceive themselves, with regard to the rigour of the tax ; it would not suffice even for the necessary expenses of the troops stationed in America : but a *pepper-corn in acknowledgment of the right is of more value than millions without*. . . . There was a time when they would not have proceeded thus; but they are now supported by the artifice of these young gentlemen; inflammatory petitions are handed about against us, and in their favor. Even within this house, in this sanctuary of the laws, sedition has found its defenders. Resistance to the laws is applauded, obstinacy encouraged, disobedience extolled, rebellion pronounced a virtue. "

In reply, William Pitt said: "Would to heaven, that my health had permitted my attendance here, when it was proposed to tax America! If my feeble voice should not have been able to avert the torrent of calamities which has fallen upon us, and the tempest which threatens us, at least my testimony would have attested that I had no part in them. It is now an act that has passed; I would speak with decency of every act of this house, but I must beg the indulgence of the house to speak of it with freedom. There is an idea in some, that the Americans are virtually represented in this house; but I would fain know by what province, county, city, or borough, they are represented here? No doubt by some province, county, city, or borough, never seen or known by them or their ancestors, and which they never will see or know. The commons of America, represented in their several assemblies, have ever been in possession of the exercise of this, their constitutional right, of giving and granting their own money. They would have been slaves if they had not enjoyed it. . . . And in our own times, even those who send no members to parliament, are all at least inhabitants of Great Britain. Many have it in their option to be actually represented. They have connections with those that elect, and they have influence over them. Would to heaven that all were better represented than they are! . . . I rejoice that America has resisted. Three millions of people, so dead to all the feelings of liberty as voluntarily to submit to be slaves, would have been fit instruments to make slaves of ourselves. . . . And shall a miserable financier come with a boast that he can fetch a pepper-corn into the exchequer to the loss of millions to the nation! . . . In such a cause, your success would be deplorable and victory hazardous. America, if she fell, would fall like a strong man. She would embrace the pillars of the state, and pull down the constitution along with her. Is this your boasted peace? . . . The Americans have not acted in all things with prudence and temper. They have been wronged. They have been driven to madness by injustice. Will you punish them for the madness you have occasioned? Rather let prudence and temper come first from the strongest side. Excuse their errors; learn to honor their virtues. Upon the whole, I will beg leave to tell the house what is really my opinion. I consider it most consistent with our dignity, most useful to our liberty, and in every respect the safest for this kingdom, that the stamp act be repealed, absolutely, totally and immediately. At the same time, let the sovereign authority . . . over the colonies be asserted in as strong terms as can be devised.

Topics for Papers.

1 State arguments used by both men.

2 What "side-light" on the sentiment of parliament in Granville's statements?

3 Did the principle in the stamp act threaten the English constitution? Prove your answer.

4 How can you reconcile the last sentence of Pitt with the rest of his speech?

XI.

MASSACHUSETTS CIRCULAR LETTER, 1768

(From British and American Papers, 191–93.)

From the house of Representatives of Massachusetts unto the speakers of the respective houses of representatives and burgesses on the continent of North America.

Sir:—

The house of representatives of this province have taken into their serious consideration the great difficulties that must accrue to themselves and their constituents by the operation of the several acts of parliament imposing duties and taxes on the American colonies. . . . They have no reason to doubt but that your house is deeply impressed with its importance, and that such constitutional measures will be come into as are proper. . . . All possible care should be taken that the representations of the several assemblies upon so delicate a point, should harmonize with each other : the house therefore hope that this letter will be candidly considered in no other light than as expressing a disposition freely to communicate their mind to a sister colony, upon a common concern, in the same manner as they would be glad to receive the sentiments of your, or any other house of representatives on the continent.

The house have humbly represented to the ministry their own sentiments: that His Majesty's high court of parliament is the supreme legislative power over the whole empire : that in a free state the constitution is fixed : and as the supreme legislative (body) derives its power and authority from the constitution, it cannot overleap the bounds of it, without destroying its foundation : that the constitution ascertains and limits both sovereignty and allegiance: and therefore His Majesty's American subjects who acknowledge themselves bound by the ties of allegiance, have an equitable claim to the full enjoyment of the fundamental rules of the British constitution: that it is an essential and unalterable right in nature, ingrafted in the British constitution as a fundamental law, and ever held sacred and irrevocable by the subjects within the realm, that what a man hath honestly acquired is absolutely his own, which he may freely give but cannot be taken from him without his consent: that the American subjects may therefore, exclusive of any consideration of charter rights, with a decent firmness adapted to the character of freemen and subjects assert this natural constitutional right. It is moreover their humble opinion . . . that the acts . . . imposing duties on the people of this province . . . are infringements of their natural and constitutional rights, because . . . His Majesty's commons in Britain by those acts grant their property without their consent.

This house further is of the opinion that their constituents . . . cannot by any possibility be represented in parliament; and that it will be forever impracticable that they should be equally represented there, and consequently not at all: . . . that His Majesty's royal predecessors, for this reason, were graciously pleased to form a subordinate legislature here, that their subjects might enjoy the unalienable right of representation. Also that . . . this house think that a taxation of their constituents, even without their consent, grievous as it is, would be preferable to any representation that could be admitted for them there. . . . Were the right of parliament ever so clear, yet . . . it would be beyond the rule of equity that their constituents should be taxed on the manufactures of Great Britain here, in addition to the duties they pay for them in England. . .

They have also submitted to consideration, whether any people can be said to enjoy any degree of freedom, if the crown in addition to its undoubted authority of constituting a governor, should appoint him such a stipend as it shall judge proper without the consent of the people, and at their expense: and whether while the judges of the land, and other civil officers, hold not their commissions during good behavior, their having salaries appointed for them by the crown, independent of the people, hath not a tendency to subvert the principles of equity and endanger the happiness and security of the subject.

. . . The house have written a letter to their agent . . . wherein they take notice of the hardship . . . which requires the governor and council to provide enumerated articles for the king's marching troops, and the people to pay the expense: and also the commission of the gentlemen appointed commissioners of the customs to reside in America, which authorizes them to make as many appointments as they think fit and to pay the appointees what sum they please. . . .

This house is fully satisfied that your assembly is too generous and enlarged in sentiment to believe that this letter proceeds from an ambition of taking the lead or of dictating to the other assemblies: they freely submit their judgment to the opinion of others ; and shall take it kind in your house to point out to them anything further that may be thought necessary.

This house cannot conclude without expressing their firm confidence in the king, our common head and father, that the united and dutiful supplications of his distressed American subjects will meet with his royal and favorable acceptance.

RESPONSE OF THE COLONIES TO THE CIRCULAR LETTER

Virginia :— They (burgesses) applaud them (Massachusetts assembly) for their attention to American liberty. . . That they do not affect an independency of their parent kingdom. . . That their ancestors brought over with them entire and transmitted to their descendants the natural and constitutional rights they had enjoyed in their native country. . . To say that the commons of Great Britain have a right to impose internal taxes on the inhabitants of this continent, who are not and cannot be represented, is in effect to bid them prepare for a state of slavery. . . The act suspending the legislative power of New York, they consider as still more alarming to the colonies, though it has that single province in view. If the parliament can compel them to furnish a single article to the troops sent over, they may, by the same rule, oblige them to furnish clothes, arms and every other necessary, even the pay of the officers and soldiers—a doctrine replete with every mischief, and utterly subversive of all that is dear and valuable. (May 9, 1768.)

Georgia:—The speaker replied in effect that the governor had prorogued the assembly till November. Hence he cannot officially convey the sentiments of the assembly, but that when it meets he says that he is "assured such measures will be pursued in consequence thereof as will manifest their regard for constitutional liberty, and their respect for the house of representatives of the province of Massachusetts Bay, whose wise and spirited conduct is so justly admired." (June 15, 1768.)

Topics for Papers.

1 Feeling toward king and reasons for it.
2 Feeling toward other colonies.
3 Rights asserted. Which are new?
4 Relation between sovereignty and allegiance.
5 Colonial representation in parliament.
6 Sentiments of the responses. What conclusions?

XII.

BOSTON TEA PARTY, 1773

1 Arrival of the tea.

The tea arrived on Sunday ; on Monday morning this hand bill was found posted :

FRIENDS ! BRETHREN ! COUNTRYMEN !

That worst of plagues, the detested TEA, shipped for this port by the East India Company, is now arrived in this harbor. The hour of destruction or manly opposition to . . . tyranny stares you in the face. Every friend to his country, to himself, and prosperity, is now called upon to meet at Faneuil Hall at nine o'clock THIS DAY (at which time the bells will ring), to make a united and successful resistance to this last, worst, and most destructive measure. . . . (*Sheldon's American History.*)

2 Extract from a tea-ship journal

Monday, Nov. 29—The captain went on shore, there being a great disturbance about the tea. A town-meeting (the largest ever known in Boston) was held, which came to a resolution the tea should never be landed. . . .

Tuesday, Nov. 30—A watch of 25 men on board this night, *to see that the tea is not landed.*

Thursday, Dec. 2—A guard of 25 men every night.

Thursday, Dec. 16—Town-meeting this day (in the Old South church, addressed by Josiah Quincy, Joseph Warren and Samuel Adams). Between six and seven o'clock this evening came down to the wharf a body of about 1000 people ; among them were a number dressed and whooping like Indians. They came on board the ship, and after warning myself and the custom-house officer to get out of the way, they . . . went down the hold, where was 80 whole and 34 half chests of tea, which they hoisted upon deck, and cut the chests to pieces, and hove the tea all overboard, where it was damaged and lost. (*Sheldon's American History.*)

3 How John Adams felt the morning after the Party.

"Last night three cargoes of tea were emptied into the sea. This morning a man of war sails. This is the most magnificent movement of all. There is a dignity, a majesty, a sublimity in this last effort of the patriots that I greatly admire. The people should never rise without doing something to be remembered—something notable and striking. This destruction of the tea is so bold, so daring, so firm, intrepid, and inflexible, and it must have so important consequences, and so lasting, that I cannot but consider it as an epoch in history.

What measures will the ministry take in consequence of this? Will they resent it? Will they dare resent it? Will they punish us? How? By quartering troops upon us? By annulling our charter? By laying on more duties? By restraining our trade? By sacrifice of individuals? Or how?

The question is whether the destruction of the tea was necessary. I apprehend it was absolutely and indispensably so. They could not send it back . . . then there was no other alternative but to destroy it or let it be landed. To let it be landed, would be giving up the principle of taxation by parliamentary authority, against which the continent has struggled for 10 years."

4 Feeling outside of Boston.

In New York "vast numbers of the people collected, and highly extolled the Bostonians." In Philadelphia the bells were rung, a large public meeting voted "the most perfect approbation, with universal huzzas;" and subsequently, when 5000 people met, they "returned their hearty thanks to the people of Boston for their resolution in destroying the tea, rather than suffering it to be landed." A letter from North Carolina said "that the deed was the only remedy left to save the colonies from slavery, and that the actors had the approbation of the whole continent."

Topics for Papers.

1 Prove that ·the tea party constituted an "epoch in history."

2 Prove that the destruction of the tea was "indispensably" necessary?

3 Prove that "the actors had the approbation of the whole continent."

4 What conclusions can be safely drawn from the "donations?"

XIII.

THE BOSTON PORT BILL, 1774.

Appeal to the colonies.

They have ordered our port to be entirely shut up, leaving us barely so much . . . as to keep us from perishing with cold and hunger; and it is said that a fleet of British ships is to block up our harbor until we shall make restitution to the East India Company for the loss of their tea. . . . The act fills the inhabitants with indignation . . . This attack, though made immediately upon us, is doubtless designed for every other colony who shall not surrender their sacred rights and liberties into the hands of an infamous ministry. Now, therefore, is the time when *all* should be united in opposition to this violation of the liberties of all.

The single question then is, whether you consider Boston as now suffering in the common cause, and sensibly feel and resent the injury and affront offered to her. If you do, and we cannot believe otherwise, may we not, from your approbation of our former conduct in defense of American liberty, rely on your suspending your trade with Great Britain at least.

Responses of the colonies.

"We feel the heavy hand of power, and claim a share of your sufferings." "Depend upon it we will further assist you with provisions and men if you need it." "Our people are open and generous, firm and resolute in the cause of liberty; hope the people of Boston remain firm and steady." "Hold on and hold out to the last. As you are placed in the front rank, if you fail all will be over." "Give us leave to entreat, to beg, to conjure you, by everything that is dear, by everything that is sacred, by the venerable names of our pious forefathers, who suffered, who bled in the defense of liberty, not to desert the cause in this trying crisis." "Stand firm, and let your intrepid courage show to the world that you are Christians."

From Fairfax co., Va., George Washington, Chairman:—"*Resolved* . . . That the inhabitants of the town of Boston are now suffering in the common cause of all British America . . . and therefore that a subscription ought immediately to be opened . . . to purchase provisions . . . to be distributed among the poorer sort of people there. . . .

"*Resolved*, That nothing will so much defeat the pernicious designs of the common enemies of Great Britain and her colonies, as a firm union of the latter, who ought to regard every act of violence or oppression inflicted upon any one . . . as aimed at all; and . . . that a congress should be appointed, to consist of deputies from all the colonies to concert . . . a plan for the defense . . . of our common rights. . . ."

Gifts received at Boston during the operation of the port bill between January 30, and April 17, 1775.

Massachusetts towns sent cash, corn, wood, rye, grain, cheese, pork, handkerchiefs (home made), meal, shoes, potatoes, turnips, cabbages, wheat, beef, rice, hay, malt, thread, moose-skin breeches, wool, tobacco, flax, shovels, spinning-wheel, flour, butter.

New Hampshire sent cash, £110.

Connecticut sent cash, sheep, cattle, cheese, corn, rye, wood, turnips, wheat, (sent in four times).

Virginia sent wheat (3723 bu.), flour, bread, corn (1525 bu. at one time; at another, over $500 worth).

New Jersey sent cash, £155.

Pennsylvania sent cash, £160, flour, (500 barrels), bar iron, nails.

Canada sent £100. Rhode Island sent cash, £221. South Carolina sent cash, £1513, and rice (80 lbs. worth). Dominica sent cocoa. Total values received, £3131.

XIV.

DECLARATION OF RIGHTS BY CONGRESS OF 1774

(American Archives, Fourth Series, Vol. I.)

On the 14th of October, the members of this congress, with unexampled unanimity, declared; "That the inhabitants of the English colonies in North America, by the immutable laws of nature, the principles of the English constitution, and the several charters or compacts, have the following rights:

1 "That they are entitled to life, liberty, and property; and they have never ceded to any sovereign power whatever, a right to dispose of either, without their consent."

2 "That our ancestors, who first settled these colonies, were, at the time of their emigration from the mother country, entitled to all the rights, liberties, and immunities, of free and natural born subjects within the realm of England."

3 "That by such emigration, they by no means

forfeited, surrendered or lost, any of those rights, but that they were, and their descendants now are, entitled to the exercise and enjoyment of all such of them, as their local and other circumstances, enable them to exercise and enjoy."

4 "That the foundation of English liberty, and of all free governments, is a right in the people to participate in their legislative council ; and as the English colonists are not represented, and from their local and other circumstances, cannot properly be represented in the British parliament, they are entitled to a free and *exclusive power of legislation*, in their several provincial legislatures, where their right of representation can only be preserved, in all cases of *taxation and internal policy*, subject only to the negative of their sovereign, in such manner as has been heretofore used and accustomed. But from the *necessity* of the case, and a regard to the mutual interest of both countries, we cheerfully consent to the operation of such acts of the British parliament, as are *bona fide*, restrained to the regulation of our external commerce, for the purpose of securing the commercial advantages of the whole empire to the mother country, and the commercial benefits of its respective members ; excluding every idea of taxation internal or external, for raising a *revenue*, on the subjects in America, without their consent."

5 "That the respective colonies, are entitled to

the common law of England, and more especially, to the great and inestimable privilege of being tried by their peers of the vicinage, according to the course of that law."

6 "That they are entitled, to the benefit of such of the English statutes, as existed at the time of their colonization; and which they have, by experience, respectively found, to be applicable to their several local and other circumstances."

7 "That these, his majesty's colonies, are likewise entitled to all the immunities and privileges granted and confirmed to them, by royal charters, or secured, by their several codes of provincial laws."

8 "That they have a right peaceably to assemble, consider of their grievances, and petition the king; and that all prosecutions, prohibitory proclamations and commitments for the same, are illegal."

9 "That the keeping a standing army in these colonies, in times of peace, without the consent of the legislature of that colony, in which such army is kept, is against law."

10 "It is indispensably necessary to good government, and rendered essential by the English constitution, that the constituent branches of the legislature, be independent of each other; that, therefore, the exercise of legislative power, in several colonies, by a council appointed during pleasure by the crown, is unconstitutional, dan-

gerous, and destructive to the freedom of American legislation."

Topics for Papers.

1 The rights asserted and the ground of the rights.

2 Are any new claims made or advanced ground taken ?

3 What facts can you give to support no. 1, 2 and 3 ?

4 Work out the points under 4 carefully.

5 Compare and contrast this declaration with that of the stamp act congress.

6 Draw inferences from these resemblances and differences.

XV.

ADDRESS TO THE PEOPLE OF GREAT BRITAIN, CONGRESS OF 1774

(American Archives, Fourth Series, Vol. 1.)

Friends and fellow subjects.—

When a nation, led to greatness by the hand of liberty, and possessed of all the glory that heroism, munificence, and humanity can bestow, descends to the ungrateful task of forging chains for her friends and children, and instead of giving support to freedom, turns advocate for slavery and oppression, there is reason to suspect she has either ceased to be virtuous, or been extremely negligent in the appointment of her rulers.

In almost every age, in repeated conflicts, in long and bloody wars, as well civil as foreign, against many and powerful nations, against the open assaults of enemies, and the more dangerous treachery of friends, have the inhabitants of your island, your great and glorious ancestors, maintained their independence, and transmitted the rights of men, and the blessings of liberty, to you, their posterity.

Be not surprised, therefore, that we, who are descended from the same common ancestors; that we, whose forefathers participated in all the rights, the liberties, and the constitution you so justly boast of, and who have carefully conveyed the same fair inheritance to us, guarantied by the plighted faith of government, and the solemn compacts with British sovereigns, should refuse to surrender them to men who found their claims on no principles of reason, and who prosecute them with a design, that by having our lives and property in their power, they may, with the greater facility, enslave you.

Know then, that we consider ourselves, and do insist that we are and ought to be, as free as our fellow subjects in Britain, and that no power on earth has a right to take our property from us, without our consent.

Are not the proprietors of the soil of GreatBritain, lords of their own property? Can it be taken from them, without their consent? Will they yield it to the arbitrary disposal of any man, or number of men whatever? You know they will not. Why then are the proprietors of the soil of America less lords of their property than you are of yours? Or why should they submit it to the disposal of your parliament or any other parliament, or council in the world, not of their election?

Reason looks with indignation on such distinctions, and freemen can never perceive their propriety. . . . Such declarations we consider as heresies in English politics, and which can no more operate to deprive us of our property, than the interdicts of the pope can divest kings of scepters which the laws of the land and the voice of the people have placed in their hands. . . . We call upon you yourselves, to witness our loyalty and attachment to the common interest of the whole empire: did we not, in the last war, add all the strength of this vast continent to the force which repelled our common enemy? Did we not leave our native shores, and meet disease and death, to promote the success of British arms in foreign climates? Did you not thank us for our zeal, and even reimburse us large sums of money, which, you confessed we had advanced beyond our proportion, and far beyond our abilities? You did. . . . Let justice and humanity cease to be the boast of your nation! Consult your history; examine your records of former transactions, nay, turn to the annals of the many arbitrary states and kingdoms that surround you, and show us a single instance of men being condemned to suffer for imputed crimes, unheard, unquestioned, and without even the specious formality of a trial; and that, too, by laws made expressly for the purpose, and which had no existence at the time of the fact committed. If it be difficult to reconcile these proceedings to the genius and temper of your laws and constitution, the task will become more arduous, when we call upon our ministerial enemies to justify, not only condemning men untried, and by hearsay, but involving the innocent in one common punishment with the guilty; and for the act of 30 or 40, to bring poverty, distress and calamity, on 30,000 souls, and those not your enemies, but your friends, brethren and fellow-subjects. . . . Nor can we suppress our astonishment, that a British parliament should ever consent to establish in that country a religion that has deluged your island in blood, and dispersed impiety, bigotry, persecution, murder, and rebellion, through every part of the world. This being a true state of facts, let us beseech you to consider to what end they lead. Admit that the ministry, by the powers of Britain, and the aid of our Roman Catholic neighbors, should be able to carry the point of taxation, and reduce us to a state of perfect humiliation and slavery; such an enterprise would doubtless make some addition to your national debt, which already presses down your liberties, and fills you with pensioners and placemen. We presume, also, that your commerce will somewhat be diminished. However, suppose you should prove victorious, in what condition will you then be? What advantages or what laurels will you reap from such a conquest?

May not a ministry with the same armies enslave you?—It may be said, you will cease to pay them; but remember the taxes from America, the wealth, and we may add the men, and particularly the Roman Catholics of this vast continent, will then be in the power of your enemies; nor will you have any reason to expect, that after making slaves of us, many among us should refuse to assist in reducing you to the same abject state. . . .

We believe there is yet much virtue, much justice, and much public spirit in the English nation. —To that justice we now appeal. You have been told that we are seditious, impatient of government, and desirous of independency. Be assured that these are not facts, but calumnies.—Permit us to be as free as yourselves, and we shall ever esteem a union with you, to be our greatest glory and our greatest happiness; we shall ever be ready to contribute all in our power to the welfare of the empire ; we shall consider your enemies as our enemies, and your interests as our own.

But, if you are determined that your ministers shall wantonly sport with the rights of mankind—if neither the voice of justice, the dictates of the law, the principles of the constitution, or the suggestions of humanity, can restrain your hands from shedding human blood, in such an impious cause, we must then tell you, that we will never submit to be hewers of wood, or drawers of water for any ministry or nation in the world.

Topics for Papers.

1 What do you infer as to the purpose of this address?

2 What sentiments does the address appeal to?

3 What sentiments must have moved the authors?

4 What warnings does it contain? Were these probable or imaginary dangers? Reasons.

5 What implications in the last two paragraphs?

XVI.

POINTS FROM SUFFOLK COUNTY RESOLVES SENT TO THE CONGRESS OF 1774

1 That the king of England is our rightful sovereign.

2 That it is our duty by all lawful means to defend our civil and religious rights and liberties.

3 That the late act for shutting the port of Boston, and for screening the most flagitious violators of the laws of the province, are gross infractions of those rights.

4 That no obedience is due from this province to either or any part of these acts, but that they ought to be rejected as the wicked attempts of an abandoned administration to establish a despotic government.

5 That so long as judges or justices of the courts are appointed, or hold places by any other tenure than that the charter directs, they must be considered as unconstitutional officers, and no regard ought to be paid to them by the people of the county.

6 That this county will support and bear harmless all sheriffs, jurors, etc. who shall fail to carry into execution the orders of said courts.

7 That it be recommended to all public offi-

cers who have public money in their hands to detain the same till the civil government of this province is placed on a constitutional foundation; or until otherwise ordered by the proposed provincial congress.

8 That those who have accepted seats at the council-board, by mandamus from the king, have violated the duties they owed their country and are advised to resign on or before the 20th of September; if not, they are to be considered as enemies to their country.

9 That the fortifications carrying on upon Boston-Neck are justly alarming to this county and more especially as the commander-in-chief has removed the powder from the magazine at Charlestown.

10 That the establishment of the Roman Catholic religion and French laws in Canada is dangerous, in the extreme, to the Protestant religion and the civil rights and liberties of all America. Therefore we are obliged to take all proper measures for our security.

11 That we ought immediately to do all in our power to perfect ourselves in the art of war and for this purpose the militia are to appear under arms once each week.

12 That during the hostile appearance of Great Britain, notwithstanding the many insults and oppressions which we feel and resent, yet from our affection to His Majesty, we are determined

to act only on the . . . defensive, so long as such conduct may be vindicated by reason and the principles of self-preservation——but no longer.

13 That we recommend that in case so audacious a measure (seizing patriot leaders) be carried into execution, all the officers of so tyrannical a government be seized and kept in safe custody till the others be restored to their friends.

14 That we recommend to withhold commercial intercourse with Great Britain.

15 That we will encourage the arts and manufactures all we can.

16 That a provincial congress ought to be called and that we recommend delegates from all the counties to meet at Concord in October.

17 That we will pay all due respect and submission to any measures the continental congress may recommend to the colonies.

18 That we recommend all orders of people to retain their resentments and avoid all riots, and that by a steady, manly, uniform and persevering opposition, to convince their enemies that in a contest so important, and in a cause so solemn, their conduct should be such as to merit the approbation of the wise and the admiration of the brave and free of every country.

(These resolutions were read in the Congress of 1774, and the answer was carried back to Boston by Paul Revere.)

Topics for papers.

1 The situation giving rise to these resolutions.

2 How do they compare in temper with the declaration of rights? Account for this difference.

3 Significance of numbers 4, 5, 6, 7, and 8. Can they be justified?

4 What new or advanced grounds are taken?

XVII.

THE CONGRESS OF 1774

Response to the Suffolk county resolves.

(American Archives, Fourth Series)

Resolved that this assembly deeply feels the sufferings of their countrymen in the Massachusetts Bay, under the operation of the late unjust, cruel, and oppressive acts of the British parliament; that we most thoroughly approve the wisdom and fortitude with which opposition to these wicked ministerial measures has hitherto been conducted, and we earnestly recommend to our brethren a perseverance in the same firm and temperate conduct, as expressed in the resolutions of the delegates for the county of Suffolk on the 6th instant;

Resolved unanimously, that contributions from all the colonies for supplying the necessities, and alleviating the distress of our brethren at Boston, ought to be continued, in such a manner, and so long as their occasion may require.

Resolved that this congress (Oct. 8) approve of the opposition made by the inhabitants of Massachusetts Bay to the execution of the late acts of parliament; and if the same shall be attempted to be carried into execution by force, in such case all America ought to support them in their opposition.

Sentiments from the congress.

George Washington wrote: "I am well satisfied that no such thing (independence) is desired by any thinking man in all North America; on the contrary, that it is the ardent wish of the warmest advocates for liberty that peace and tranquillity, on constitutional grounds, may be restored, and the horrors of civil discord prevented."

John Adams wrote: "If it is the secret hope of many, as I suspect it is, that the congress will advise to offensive measures, they will be mistaken. I have had opportunities enough, both public and private, to learn with certainty the decisive sentiments of the delegates and others on this point. They will not at this session vote to raise men or money, or arms or ammunition. Their opinions are fixed against hostilities, and rupture, except they should become absolutely necessary ; and this necessity they do not yet see. They dread the thought of an action, because it would make a wound which would never be healed ; it would establish a rancor which would descend to the latest generations ; it would render all hope of a reconciliation with Great Britain desperate ; it would light up the flames of war, perhaps through the whole continent, which might rage for 20 years, and result in the subduction of America as likely as her liberation."

Patrick Henry said he hoped "that future ages would quote their proceedings with applause." "British oppression has effaced the boundaries of the several colonies; the distinctions between Virginians, Pennsylvanians, New Yorkers, and New Englanders are no more. I am not a Virginian, but an American."

Richard Henry Lee : "Our ancestors found here no government; and as a consequence had a right to make their own. Charters are an unsafe reliance, for the king's right to grant them has itself been denied. Besides the right to life and the right to liberty are inalienable."

Galloway wrote: "Samuel Adams, though by no means remarkable for brilliant abilities, is equal to most men in popular intrigue, and in the management of a faction. He eats little, drinks little, sleeps little, and thinks much, and is most decisive and indefatigable in the pursuit of his objects. He was the man who, by his superior application managed at once the faction in congress at Philadelphia and the faction in New England."

Topics for Papers.

Draw conclusions about the following:

1 Approving the conduct of Boston by congress.

2 Recommendations to America.

3 Attitude of congress toward resistance and independence.

4 Historical significance of Henry's and Lee's sentiments.

XVIII.

PREPARATION FOR THE CONFLICT

(Extracts of a letter from Philadelphia, Dec. 24, 1774, to a member of Parliament.)

(American Archives, Fourth Series, Vol. I.)

"The proclamation (to prevent export of powder and guns to America) will be rendered ineffectual by a manufactory of gunpowder . . . the materials of which may be procured in great perfection among ourselves. . . . There are moreover gunsmiths enough in the province to make 100,000 stands of arms in one year. . . . Such is the wonderful martial spirit which is enkindled among us, that we begin to think the whole force of Great Britain could not subdue us. . . . The four New England colonies, together with Virginia and Maryland, are completely armed and disciplined. The province of Pennsylvania will follow their example in a few weeks. Our militia will amount to not less than 60,000 men. Nothing but a total repeal of the acts of parliament of which we complain can prevent a civil war in America. Our opposition has now arisen to desperation. It would be as easy to allay a storm in the ocean by a single word, as to subdue the free spirit of Americans, without a total redress of their grievances. . . . We tremble at the thought of a separation from Great Britain. All our glory and happiness have been derived from you. But we are in danger of being shipwrecked upon your rocks. To avoid these, we are willing to be tossed, without compass or guide, for a while upon an ocean of blood. . . ."

On Dec. 26, the same writer continues : "There cannot be a greater error than to suppose that the present commotions in America are owing to the arts of demagogues. Every man thinks and acts for himself. . . . It is to no purpose to attempt to destroy the opposition to the omnipotence of parliament by taking off our Hancocks, Adamses and Dickinsons. Ten thousand patriots of the same stamp stand ready to fill their places. Would to Heaven our rulers would consider these things in time. . . . For God's sake try to rouse up the ancient spirit of the nation. We love you—we honor you as brethren and fellow subjects. We have shared in your dangers and glories. Only grant us the liberty you enjoy, and we shall always remain one people. Let the bond of our union be in the crown of Great Britain."

Fairfax county, Va., Washington in the chair, voted, Feb. 2, 1775, a tax for the purchase of arms, etc., and to enroll the inhabitants from 16 to 60 years of age, and to practice military exercise.

Before the Virginia convention of delegates, in March, 1775, Patrick Henry introduced and carried the following: "Resolved that this colony be put immediately into a state of of defense, and that a committee be appointed to prepare a plan for embodying, arming, and disciplining such a number of men as may be sufficient for that purpose."

General Charles Lee said: "I have now run through the whole of the colonies from the North to the South. I have conversed with every order of men, from the first-estated gentlemen to the poorest planters, and cannot express my astonishment at the unanimity, and ardent spirit reigning through the whole. They are determined to sacrifice everything . . . their property, their wives, children, and blood . . . rather than cede a tittle of what they conceive to be their rights."

John Dickinson: "The first act of violence on the part of the administration in America will put its whole continent in arms from Nova Scotia to Georgia."

Topics for Papers.

Points to discover:

1 Geographical extent of the military preparations.

2 Nature of the preparations.

3 What sentiments moved the author of the letter? Were these sentiments individual or general? Prove your answer from the document.

4 Whether these extracts point to resistance or independence. Cite facts to prove your conclusion.

XIX.

EFFECTS OF THE CONGRESS OF 1774 ON ENGLAND

(Extracts from Lord Chatham's motion and speech.)

That an humble address be presented to his

majesty, to advise and beseech (most humbly) . . . that . . . to open the way towards an happy settlement of the dangerous troubles in America . . . and, above all, for preventing any sudden and fatal catastrophe at Boston. . . . orders may be dispatched to General Gage for removing His Majesty's forces from the town of Boston.

My lords, these papers from America, now laid by administration for the first time before your lordships have been to my certain knowledge five or six weeks in the pocket of the minister. And notwithstanding the fate of this kingdom hangs on the event of this great controversy, we are but this moment (Jan. 20, 1775) called to a consideration of this important subject. . . . I do not wish to look into these papers. . . . I know there is not a member . . . but is well acquainted with their purport, also. We ought to proceed immediately. We ought to seize the first moment to open the door of reconciliation. The Americans will never be in a temper or state to be reconciled ; they ought not to be, till the troops are withdrawn. . . . I know not who advised the present measures : . . . but this I will say, that whoever advises them, ought to answer for it, at his utmost peril. I know that no one will avow that he advised, or that he was the author of these measures ; every one shrinks from the charge. . . . His Majesty may indeed wear his crown, but, the American Jewel out of it, it will not be worth the wearing. . . . I must not say, the king is betrayed ; but this I will say, the nation is ruined. . . .

They say you have no right to tax them without their consent. They say truly. Representation and taxation must go together ; they are inseparable. Yet there is scarcely a man in our streets, though so poor, as scarcely to be able to get his daily bread, but thinks he is the legislator of America. '*Our American subjects*' is a common phrase in the mouths of the lowest orders of our citizens ; but property, my lords, is the sole and entire dominion of the owner : it excludes all the world besides the owner. None can intermeddle with it. It is a unity, a mathematical point. It is an atom ; untangible by any but the proprietor. . . . But how have this respectable people behaved, under their grievances ? With unexampled patience, with unparalleled wisdom. They chose delegates, by their free suffrages ; no bribery, no corruption, no influence there, my lords. Their representatives meet, with the sentiments and temper, and speak the sense of the continent. For genuine sagacity, for singular moderation, for solid wisdom, manly spirit, sublime sentiments, and simplicity of language, for everything respectable, and honorable, the congress of Philadelphia shine unrivalled. This wise people speak out. They do not hold the language of slaves ; they tell you what they mean. They do not ask you to repeal your laws, as a *favor;* they claim it, as a *right*—they demand it. They tell you they will not submit to them; and I tell you, the acts must be repealed; they will be repealed; you cannot enforce them.

My lords, deeply impressed with the importance of taking some healing measures, at this most alarming, distracted state of our affairs, though bowed down with a cruel disease, I have crawled to this house to give you my best council and experience. . .

XX.

EXTRACTS FROM "COMMON SENSE"

(Published January 9, 1776)

(Frothingham's Republic, 472–478)

I offer nothing more than simple facts, plain arguments, and common sense. The period of debate is closed. Arms, as the last recourse, decide the contest. The appeal was the choice of the king, and the continent hath accepted the challenge. . . . 'Tis not the affair of a city, a county, a province, or a kingdom, but of a continent,—of at least one-eighth part of the habitable globe. 'Tis not the concern of a day, a year, or an age: posterity are virtually involved in the contest, and will be more or less affected, even to the end of time, by the proceedings now. . . . Britain is the parent country, say some. Then the more shame for her conduct. Europe, not England, is the parent country of America. This new world hath been the asylum for the persecuted lovers of civil and religious liberty from every part of Europe. The same tyranny which drove the first emigrants from home pursues their descendants still. We claim brotherhood with every European Christian, and triumph in the generosity of the sentiment.

I challenge the warmest advocate for reconciliation to shew a single advantage that this continent can reap by being connected with Great Britain. Everything that is right or reasonable pleads for separation. The blood of the slain, the weeping voice of Nature cries, 'Tis time to part. Even the distance at which the Almighty hath placed England and America is a strong and natural proof that the authority of the one over the other was never the design of Heaven. Men of passive tempers look somewhat lightly over the offenses of Britain, and, still hoping for the best, are apt to call out, 'Come, come! we shall be friends again for all this.' But examine the passions and feelings of mankind, bring the doctrine of reconciliation to the touchstone of nature, and then tell me whether you can hereafter love, honor, and faithfully serve the power that hath carried fire and sword into your land? If you cannot do all these, then are you only deceiving yourselves, and by your delay bringing ruin on posterity. But if you say you can pass the violations over, then I ask, hath your house been burnt? hath your property been destroyed before your face? have you lost a parent or child by their hands, and yourself the ruined and wretched survivor? If you have not, then you are not a judge of those who have. But if you have, and can still shake hands with the murderer, then are you unworthy the name of husband, father, friend, or lover; and, whatever may be your rank and title in life, you have the heart of a coward and the spirit of a sycophant. 'Tis not in the power of England or of Europe to conquer America.

But the most powerful of all arguments is, that nothing but independence—i. e., a continental form of government—can keep the peace of the continent, and preserve it inviolate from civil wars. . . . I have heard some men say that they dreaded independence, fearing that it would produce civil wars. The colonies have manifested such a spirit of good order and obedience to continental government as is sufficient to make every reasonable person easy and happy on that head. . . . Can we but leave posterity with a settled form of government, an independent constitution of its own, the purchase at any price will be cheap.

Under our present denomination of British subjects, we can neither be received nor heard abroad: the custom of all courts is against us, and will be so until by an independence we take rank with other nations. These proceedings may at first appear strange and difficult, but, like all other steps which we have passed over, will in a little time become familiar and agreeable.

Topics for Papers.

1 What battles had already occurred?

2 Select and number the arguments for independence.

3 Are these such as would appeal to the people at this time? Prove your answer.

4 How far back in time would public sentiment have sustained these arguments?

5 Do they appeal to common sense?

XXI.

POLITICAL DOCTRINES OF THE DECLARATION OF INDEPENDENCE

When, in the course of human events, it becomes necessary for one people to dissolve the political bands which have connected them with another, and to assume, among the powers of the earth, the separate and equal station to which the laws of nature and nature's God entitle them, a decent respect for the opinions of mankind requires that they should declare the causes which impel them to the separation.

We hold these truths to be self-evident--that all men are created equal; that they are endowed by their Creator with certain unalienable rights; that among these are life, liberty, and the pursuit of happiness; that, to secure these rights, governments are instituted among men, deriving their just powers from the consent of the governed; that whenever any form of government becomes destructive of these ends, it is the right of the people to alter or to abolish it, and to institute new governments, laying its foundation on such principles, and organizing its powers in such form, as to them shall seem most likely to effect their safety and happiness. Prudence, indeed, will dictate, that governments, long established, should not be changed for light and transient causes; and accordingly all experience hath shown, that mankind are more disposed to suffer, while evils are sufferable, than to right themselves by abolishing the forms to which they are accustomed. But when a long train of abuses and usurpations, pursuing invariably the same object, evinces a design to reduce them under absolute despotism, it is their right, it is their duty to throw off such government, and to provide new guards for their future security. Such has been the patient sufferance of these colonies ; and such is now the necessity which constrains them to alter their former systems of government. The history of the present king of Great Britain is a history of repeated injuries and usurpations, all having in direct object the establishment of an absolute tyranny over these states. . . .

We, therefore, the representatives of the United States of America, in general congress assembled, appealing to the Supreme Judge of the world, for the rectitude of our intentions, do, in the name and by the authority of the good people of these colonies, solemnly publish and declare, that these united colonies are, and of right ought to be, free and independent states ; that they are absolved from all allegiance to the British crown, and that all political connection between them and the state of Great Britain is and ought to be totally dissolved ; and that as free and independent states, they have full power to levy war, conclude peace, contract alliances, establish commerce, and to do all other acts and things which independent states may of right do. And for the support of this declaration, with a firm reliance on the protection of Divine Providence, we mutually pledge to each other our lives, our fortunes, and our sacred honor.

Topics for Papers

1 List the likenesses and differences between the declaration of rights and the declaration of independence.

2 Analyze the first part of the declaration of independence into its political principles.

3 What is the logical connection between the parts of the declaration?

4 What degree of sovereignty is expressed in the last portion of the declaration?

Documents on Origin of the Constitution

XXII.

COLONEL HAMILTON TO THE HON. JAMES DUANE

(Hamilton, *Life of Hamilton*, *v.* 1.)

Liberty Pole, 1780.

Dear Sir:—The fundamental defect is a want of power in congress . . . it has originated from three causes: an excess of the spirit of liberty, which has made the particular states show a jealousy of all power not in their own hands; . . . a diffidence in congress of their own powers, by which they have been . . . indecisive in their resolutions, constantly making concessions to the states; a want of sufficient means . . . to answer the public exigencies, and of vigor to draw forth those means which have occasioned them to depend on the states.

. . . The manner in which congress was appointed would warrant that they should have considered themselves as vested with full power *to preserve the republic from harm.*

They have done many of the highest acts of sovereignty which were always cheerfully submitted to.

. . . The idea of an uncontrollable sovereignty in each state, will defeat the other powers given to congress, and make our union feeble and precarious . . .

There is a wide difference between our situation and that of an empire under one simple form of government, distributed into counties, provinces or districts which have no legislatures, but merely magistratical bodies to execute the laws of a common sovereign. Here the danger is, that the sovereign will have too much power and oppress the parts of which it is composed. In our case, that of an empire composed of confederative states, each with a government completely organized within itself, having all the means to draw its subjects to a close dependence on itself, the danger is directly the reverse. It is that the common sovereign will not have power sufficient to unite the different members together, and direct the common forces to the interest and happiness of the whole.

. . . We have felt the difficulty of drawing out the resources of the country, and inducing the states to combine in equal exertions for the common cause.

Lately, congress convinced of these inconveniences, have gone into the measure of appointing boards. . . .

A single man in each department of the administration would be greatly preferable. It would give us a chance of more knowledge, more activity, more responsibility, and of course more zeal and attention. . . .

A third defect is the fluctuating constitution of our army. All our military misfortunes, three fourths of our civil embarrassments, are to be ascribed to it. . . .

The imperfect and unequal provision made for the army, is a fourth defect. Without a speedy change, the army must dissolve; it is now a mob rather than an army, without clothing, without pay, without provision, without morals, without discipline. We begin to hate the country for its neglect of us; the country begins to hate us for our oppressions of them. Congress have long been jealous of us, we have now lost all confidence of them, and give the worst construction to all they do. . . .

The first step must be to give congress powers competent to the public exigencies. This may happen in two ways: one by resuming and exercising the discretionary powers I suppose to have been originally vested in them for the safety of the states; the other by calling immediately a convention of all the states, with full authority to conclude finally upon a general confederation of all the states.

. . . The first plan, I expect will be thought too bold an expedient by the generality of congress. . . I see no objection to the other mode. . . A convention may agree upon a confederation; the states, individually, hardly ever will. We must have one, at all events, and a vigorous one, if we mean to succeed in the contest and be happy hereafter. . . I ask that the convention should have a power of vesting the whole or a part of the unoccupied lands in congress, because it is necessary that body should have some property, as a fund for the arrangements of finance.

The confederation, in my opinion, should give congress a complete sovereignty; except as to that part of internal police which relates to the rights of property and life among individuals, and to raising money by internal taxes. . .

The second step I would recommend is that congress should instantly appoint the following great officers of state: a secretary of foreign affairs; a president of war; a president of marine; a financier; a president of trade. . . These officers should have nearly the same powers and functions as those in France analogous to them, and each should be chief in his department. . .

Another step of immediate necessity is to recruit the army for the war or at least for three years. . . The placing the officers upon half pay during life would be a great stroke of policy, and would give congress a stronger tie upon them than anything else they can do. . .

And why cannot we have an American bank? Are our moneyed men less enlightened to their own interest, or less enterprising in the pursuit? I believe the fault is in government, which does not exert itself to engage them in such a scheme. . .

And in future, my dear sir, two things let me recommend, as fundamental rules for the conduct of congress; to attach the army to them by every motive, to maintain an authority (not domineering), in all their measures with the states.

Topics for Papers.

1 The fundamental defect of the confederation.
  a What was it, and what were its causes?
  b Can you name a defect more fundamental still?

2 What was the difference between the danger of a monarchy and that of the confederation? Prove that this was or was not true then of England and America.

3 Name and number the defects of the confederation as seen by Hamilton.

4 Name and number his remedies.

5 Which of these have been applied?

6 Did the remedies look toward state sovereignty or toward nationality? Explain in general terms.

XXIII.

THE VIRGINIA PLAN.

(Bancroft, *Constitution.*)

"The articles of confederation ought to be so corrected and enlarged as to accomplish the objects proposed by their institution; namely, 'common defense, security of liberty and general welfare.'

"The rights of suffrage in the national legislature ought to be proportioned to the quotas of contribution or to the number of free inhabitants.

"The national legislature ought to consist of two branches, of which the members of the first or democratic house ought to be elected by the people of the several states; of the second, by those of the first, out of persons nominated by the individual legislatures.

"The national legislature, of which each branch ought to possess the right of originating acts, ought to enjoy the legislative rights vested in congress by the confederation, and moreover to legislate in all cases to which the separate states are incompetent, or in which the harmony of the United States might be interrupted by the exercise of individual legislation; to negative all laws passed by the several states contravening the articles of union; and to call forth the force of the union against any member of the union failing to fulfill its duty under the articles thereof.

"A national executive, chosen by the national legislature and ineligible a second time, ought to enjoy the executive rights vested in congress by the confederation and a general authority to execute the national laws.

"The executive and a convenient number of the national judiciary ought to compose a council of revision, with authority to examine every act of the national legislature before it shall operate.

"A national judiciary ought to be established, to consist of supreme and inferior tribunals, to be chosen by the national legislature; to hold their offices during good behavior, with jurisdiction to hear and determine all piracies and felonies on the high seas; captures from an enemy; cases in which foreigners and citizens, a citizen of one state and a citizen of another state may be interested; cases which respect the collection of the national revenue; impeachments of national officers; and questions which may involve the national peace and harmony.

"Provision ought to be made for the admission of states lawfully arising within the limits of the United States.

"A republican government, and the territory of each state ought to be guaranteed by the United States to each state.

"Provision ought to be made for the completion of all the engagements of congress, and for its continuance until after the articles of union shall have been adopted.

"Provision ought to be made for the amendment of the articles of union, to which the assent of the national legislature ought not to be required.

"The legislative, executive and judiciary powers, within the several states, ought to be bound by oath to support the articles of union.

"The amendments which shall be offered to the confederation by the convention, ought, after the approbation of congress, to be submitted to assemblies of representatives, recommended by the several legislatures to be expressly chosen by the people to consider and decide thereon."

Topics for Papers.

1 Are these propositions for a new constitution or for amendments? Prove by a quotation.

2 Are the changes fundamental or incidental? Prove.

3 Which of these points were incorporated in our constitution?

4 Which did not become a part of our constitution?

5 Which imply a government based on state sovereignty? Which on national sovereignty?

XXIV.

THE LEADING POINTS FROM THE NEW JERSEY PLAN

(Elliot, *Debates*, v. 5, p. 191.)

1 That the articles of confederation ought to be revised, corrected and enlarged.

2 That congress have these additional powers:
   a To raise a revenue.
   b To regulate foreign trade.
   c All violations of above powers to be tried by state courts.

3 That requisitions be made in proportion to the whole number of white and other free citizens, and inhabitants of every age, sex and condition, including those bound to servitude for a term of years, and three fifths of all other persons, except Indians not paying taxes.

4 That the United States in congress be authorized to elect a federal executive.

5 That a federal judiciary be established, to

consist of a supreme tribunal, the judges of which shall be appointed by the executive and hold their offices during good behavior.

6 That all acts of the United States in congress, and all treaties made and ratified under the authority of the United States shall be the supreme law of the states, so far as those acts or treaties shall relate to the said states or their citizens.

a The judiciary of the several states shall be bound thereby in their decisions.

b In case of opposition from any state or body of men in any state toward such acts or treaties, the federal executive shall be authorized to call forth the power of the states to enforce obedience.

7 That provision be made for the admission of new states into the union.

8 That the rule for naturalization ought to be the same in every state.

9 That a citizen of one state, committing an offense in another state of the union, shall be deemed guilty of the same offense as if it had been committed by a citizen of the state in which the offense was committed.

Topics for Papers.

1 State the resemblances between this and the Virginia plan.

2 State the differences.

3 What conclusions, in the light of this comparison and contrast ?

XXV.

HAMILTON'S IDEAS OF A CONSTITUTION

(Elliot, *Debates*, v. 5, p. 205.)

(The following was meant only to give a more correct view of his ideas, and to suggest the amendments which he should probably propose to the plan of Mr. Randolph, in the proper stages of its future discussion.)

1 "The supreme legislative power of the United States of America to be vested in two different bodies of men ; the one to be called the assembly ; the other the senate ; who, together, shall form the legislature of the United States, with power to pass all laws whatsoever, subject to the negative hereafter mentioned.

2 "The assembly to consist of persons elected by the people to serve for three years.

3 "The senate to consist of persons elected to serve during good behavior; their election to be made by electors chosen for that purpose by the people. In order to do this, the states to be divided into election districts. On the death, removal, or resignation of any senator, his place to be filled out of the district from which he came.

4 "The supreme executive authority of the United States to be vested in a governor, to be elected to serve during good behavior; the election to be made by electors chosen by the people in the election districts aforesaid. The authorities and functions of the executive to be as follows: to have a negative on all laws about to be passed, and the execution of all laws passed; to have the direction of war when authorized or begun; to have with the advice and approbation of the senate, the power of making all treaties; to have the sole appointment of the heads or chief officers of the departments of finance, war, and foreign affairs; to have the nomination of all other officers (ambassadors to foreign nations included), subject to the approbation of the senate; to have the power of pardoning all offenses except treason, which he shall

not pardon without the approbation of the senate.

5 "On the death, resignation, or removal of the governor, his authorities to be exercised by the president of the senate till a successor be appointed.

6 "The senate to have sole power of declaring war; the power of advising and approving all treaties; the power of approving or rejecting all appointments of officers, except the heads or chiefs of the departments of finance, war, and foreign affairs.

7 "The supreme judicial authority to be vested in judges, to hold their offices during good behavior with adequate and permanent salaries. This court to have original jurisdiction in all cases of capture, and an appellate jurisdiction in all causes in which the revenues of the general government, or the citizens of foreign nations are concerned.

8 "The legislature of the United States to have power to institute courts in each state for the determination of all matters of general concern.

9 "The governor, senators, and all officers of the United States to be liable to impeachment for mal and corrupt conduct; and, upon conviction, to be removed from office and disqualified for holding any

place of trust or profit; all impeachments to be tried by a court to consist of the chief, or judge of the superior court of each state, provided such judge shall hold his place during good behavior and have a permanent salary.

10 "All laws of the particular states contrary to the constitution or laws of the United States to be utterly void and, the better to prevent such laws being passed, the governor or president of each state shall be appointed by the general government, and shall have a negative upon the laws about to be passed in the state of which he is the governor or president.

11 "No state to have any forces, land or naval; and the militia of all the states to be under the sole and exclusive direction of the United States, the officers of which to be appointed and commissioned by them."

Topics for Papers.

1 Which of these topics are partly covered by the Virginia plan?

2 What parts are found in our present constitution?

3 Enumerate the points not incorporated in our present constitution.

4 Which of these points omitted would have

centralized power more than it is? Do these points justify the charge that Hamilton favored a monarchy?

XXVI.

SPEECHES ON THE CONNECTICUT COMPROMISE.

(Eliot, *Debates,* v. 5.)

Mr Ellsworth moved: "that the rule of suffrage in the second branch be the same with that established by the articles of confederation." He was not sorry, on the whole, he said, that the vote just passed had determined against this rule in the first branch. He hoped it would become a ground of compromise with regard to the second branch. We were partly national, partly federal. The proportional representation in the first branch was conformable to the national principle, and would secure the large states against the small. An equality of voices was conformable to the federal principle, and was necessary to secure the small states against the large. He trusted that on this middle ground a compromise would take place. He did not see that it could on any other, and if no compromise should take place, our meeting would not only be in vain, but worse than vain. . . . The large states, he conceived, would, notwithstanding the equality of votes, have an influence that would maintain their superiority. Holland, as had been admitted (by Mr. Madison), had, notwithstanding a like equality in the Dutch confederacy, a prevailing influence in the public measures. The power of self-defense was essential to the small states. Nature had given it to the smallest insect of creation. He could never admit that there was no danger of combinations among the large states. They will, like individuals, find out and avail themselves of the advantage to be gained by it. A defensive combination of the small states was rendered more difficult by their greater number. He would mention another consideration of great weight. The existing confederation was founded on the equality of the states in the article of suffrage,—was it meant to pay no regard to this antecedent plighted faith? Let a strong executive, a judiciary, and legislative power be created, but let not too much be attempted, by which all may be lost. He was not in general a half-way man, yet he preferred doing half the good we could, rather than do nothing at all. (p. 260.)

Mr. Madison. He entreated the gentlemen representing the small states to renounce a principle which was confessedly unjust, which could never be admitted, and which, if admitted, must infuse mortality into a constitution which we wished to last forever. He prayed them to ponder well the consequence of suffering the confederacy to go to pieces. It had been said that the want of energy in the large states would be a security to the small. It was forgotten that this want of energy proceeded from the supposed security of the states against all external danger. Let each state depend on itself for its security, and let apprehensions arise of danger from distant powers or from neighboring states, and the languishing condition of all the states, large as well as small, would soon be transformed into vigorous and high-toned governments. His great fear was, that their governments would then have too much energy; that this might not only be formidable in the large to the small states, but fatal to the internal liberty of all. The same causes which have rendered the old world the theatre of incessant wars, and have banished liberty from the face of it, would soon produce the same effects here.

Topics for Papers

1 Enumerate briefly the arguments of Ellsworth.

2 State concisely the points made by Madison.

3 What political principles were in conflict, and how were the states divided on them?

4 Did this compromise prevent the formation of parties on basis of size of states? Reasons.

XXVII.

FIRST DISCUSSIONS ON THE EXECUTIVE

(Elllot, *Debates*, v. 5, p. 140–416, 14)

Friday, June 1.

The committee of the whole proceeded to the seventh resolution, that a national executive be instituted, etc.

Mr. Pinckney was for a vigorous executive, but was afraid the executive powers of the existing congress might extend to peace and war, etc.; which would render the executive a monarchy of the worst kind, to wit, an elective one.

Mr. Wilson moved that the executive consist of a single person. Mr. C. Pinckney seconded the motion, so as to read, "that a national executive, to consist of a single person, be instituted."

A considerable pause ensuing, and the chairman asking if he should put the question, Dr. Franklin observed, that it was a point of great importance and wished the gentlemen would deliver their sentiments on it before the question was put.

Mr. Sherman said he considered the executive magistracy as nothing more than an institution for carrying the will of the legislature into effect; that the person or persons ought to be appointed by, and accountable to, the legislature only, which was the depository of the supreme will of the society. As they were the best judges of the business which ought to be done by the executive department, and consequently of the number necessary from time to time for doing it, he wished the number might not be fixed, but that the legislature should be at liberty to appoint one or more, as experience might dictate.

Mr. Wilson preferred a single magistrate, as giving most energy, despatch and responsibility to the office. He did not consider the prerogatives of the British monarch as a proper guide in defining the executive powers. Some of these prerogatives were of a legislative nature ; among others, that of war and peace, etc . . . .

Mr. Gerry favored the policy of annexing a council to the executive, in order to give weight and inspire confidence.

Mr. Randolph strenuously opposed a unity in the executive magistracy. He regarded it as the fetus of monarchy. We had, he said, no motive to be governed by the British government as our prototype. He did not mean, however, to throw censure on that excellent fabric. If we were in a situation to copy it, he did not know that he should be opposed to it ; but the fixed genius of the people of America required a different form of government. He could not see why the great requisites for the executive department,—vigor, despatch and responsibility,—could not be found in three men, as well as in one man. The executive ought to be independent. It ought, therefore, in order to support its independence, to consist of more than one.

Mr. Wilson's motion for a single magistrate was postponed by common consent, the committee seeming unprepared for any decision on it, and the first part of the clause agreed to, viz., "that a national executive be instituted."

Dr. Franklin. "It will be said, that we don't propose to establish kings. I know it; but there is a natural inclination in mankind to kingly government. It sometimes relieves them from aristocratic domination. They had rather have one tyrant than 500. It gives more of the appearance of equality among citizens, and that they like. I am apprehensive, therefore, perhaps too apprehensive, that the government of these states may in future times end in a monarchy. But this catastrophe I think may be long delayed, if in our proposed system we do not sow seeds of contention, faction, and tumult, by making our posts of honor places of profit. If we do, I fear that, though we do at first employ a number, and not a single person, the number will in time be set aside; it will only nourish the fetus of a king, as the honorable gentleman from Virginia very aptly expressed it, and a king will the sooner be set over us."

Patrick Henry (before Virginia convention).

"When the American spirit was in its youth, the language of America was different : *liberty*, sir, was *then* the *primary object*. And again, this constitution is said to have beautiful features ; but when I come to examine these features, sir, they appear to me horribly frightful ; among other deformities, it has an *awful squinting ; it squints toward monarchy*. And does not this raise indignation in the heart of every true American ? Your president may easily become king. . . *If your American chief be a man of ambition and abilities, how easy is it for him to render himself absolute. The army is in his hands : and if he be a man of address, it will be attached to him ; and it will be the subject of long meditation with him to seize the first auspicious moment to accomplish his design ; and, sir, will the American spirit, solely, relieve you when this happens ?* I would rather *infinitely*, and I am sure most of this convention are of the same opinion, have a king, lords, and commons, than a government so replete with such insupportable evils. If we make a king, we may prescribe the rules by which he shall rule his people, and interpose such checks as shall prevent him from infringing them ; *but the president in the field, at the head of his army, can prescribe the terms on which he shall reign master, so far that it will puzzle any American ever to get his neck from under the galling yoke.*" (Wirt, *Life of Patrick Henry*, pp. 279–81.)

Topics for Papers.

1 How many and what different kinds of executives are here suggested?

2 What different relations to legislative departments are suggested?

3 Who opposed a vigorous executive and on what grounds? Has this danger ever threatened our government?

4 What men came nearest our executive in their notions?

XXVIII.

SENTIMENTS FROM THE CONVENTION

(Elliot, *Debates*, v. 5,)

Mr. Wilson. The British government cannot be our model. We have no materials for a similar one. Our manners, our laws, the abolition of entails and of primogeniture, the whole genius of the people, are opposed to it. He did not see the danger of the states being devoured by the national government. On the contrary, he wished to keep them from devouring the national government. (Elliot, *Debates*, v. 5, p. 168–69.)

Mr. Gerry insisted, that the commercial and moneyed interest would be more secure in the hands of the state legislatures than of the people at large. The former have more sense of character, and will be restrained by that from injustice. The people are for paper money, when the legislatures are against it. (p. 169.)

Mr. Pinckney moved, "that the national legislature should have authority to negative all laws which they should judge to be improper." (pp. 170–71.)

Mr. Madison seconded the motion. He could not but regard an indefinite power to negative legislative acts of the states as absolutely necessary to a perfect system. (p. 171.)

Dr. Franklin. "Sir, there are two passions which have a powerful influence on the affairs of men. These are ambition and avarice; the love of power, and the love of money. Separately, each of these has great force in prompting men to action; but when united in view of the same object, they have in many minds the most violent effects. Place before the eyes of such men a post of honor, that shall be at the same time a place of profit, and they will move heaven and earth to get it. The vast number of such places it is that renders the British government so tempestuous. The struggles for them are the true sources of all those factions which are perpetually dividing the nation, distracting its councils, hurrying sometimes into fruitless and mischievous wars, and often compelling a submission to dishonorable terms of peace." (p. 145.)

Colonel Mason. Under the existing confederacy, congress represents the states, and not the people of the states; their acts operate on the states, not on the individuals. The case will be changed in the new plan of government. The people will be represented; they ought, therefore, to choose the representatives. (p. 161.)

Mr. Dickinson considered the business as so important that no man ought to be silent or reserved. He went into a discourse of some length, the sum of which was, that the legislative, executive, and judiciary departments ought to be made as independent as possible; but that such an executive as some seemed to have in contemplation was not consistent with a republic; that a firm executive could only exist in a limited monarchy. In the British government itself, the weight of the executive arises from the attachments which the crown draws to itself, and not merely from the force of its prerogatives. In place of these attachments, we must look out for something else. One source of stability is the double branch of the legislature. The division of the country into distinct states formed the other principal source of stability. This division ought, therefore, to be maintained, and considerable powers to be left with the states. This was the ground of his consolation for the future fate of his country. Without this, and in case of a consolidation of the states into one great republic, we might read its fate in the history of smaller ones. (p. 148.)

Mr. Butler had been in favor of a single executive magistrate; but could he have entertained an idea that a complete negative on the laws was to be given him, he certainly should have acted very differently. It had been observed that in all countries the executive power is in a constant course of increase. This was certainly the case in Great Britain. But why might not a Catiline or a Cromwell arise in this country as well as in others? (p. 153.)

Mr. Bedford. The little states are willing to observe their engagements, but will meet the large ones on no ground but that of confederation. We have been told, with a dictatorial air, that this is the last moment for a fair trial in favor of a good government. It will be the last, indeed, if the propositions reported from the committee go forth to the people. The large states dare not dissolve the confederation. If they do, the small ones will find some foreign ally, of more honor and good faith, who will take them by the hand, and do them justice. (p. 268.)

Mr. Pinckney moved to amend Mr. Randolph's motion, so as to make "blacks equal to the whites in the ratio of representation." This, he urged, was nothing more than justice. The blacks are the laborers, the peasants of the southern states. They are as productive of pecuniary resources as those of the northern states. (p. 305.)

Gen. Pinckney declared it to be his firm opinion

that if himself and all his colleagues were to sign the constitution and use their personal influence, it would be of no avail towards obtaining the assent of their constituents. South Carolina and Georgia cannot do without slaves.

Mr. Davie said it was high time now to speak out. He saw that it was meant by some gentlemen to deprive the southern states of any share of representation for their blacks. He was sure that North Carolina would never confederate on any terms that did not rate them at least at three-fifths. If the eastern states meant, therefore, to exclude them altogether, the business was at an end. (p. 303.)

Mr. Sherman said it was better to let the southern states import slaves than to part with them, if they made that a *sine qua non.* He was opposed to a tax on slaves imported, as making the matter worse, because it implied they were property. (p. 461.)

Mr. Gouverneur Morris. He never would concur in upholding domestic slavery. . . . It was the curse of heaven on the states where it prevailed. Compare the free regions of the middle states, where a rich and noble cultivation marks the prosperity and happiness of the people, with the misery and poverty which overspreads the barren wastes of Virginia, Maryland, and the other states having slaves. . . Upon what principle is it that slaves shall be computed in the representation? Are they men? Then make them citizens, and let them vote. Are they property? Why, then, is no other property included? . . . The admission of slaves into the representation, when fairly explained, comes to this: That the inhabitant of Georgia and South Carolina who goes to the coast of Africa, and, in defiance of the most sacred laws of humanity, tears away his fellow-creatures from their dearest connections, and damns them to the most cruel bondage, shall have more votes, in a government instituted for the protection of the rights of mankind, than the citizen of Pennsylvania or New Jersey, who views, with a laudable horror, so nefarious a practice. . . Domestic slavery is the most prominent feature in the aristocratic countenance of the proposed constitution. The vassalage of the poor has ever been the favorite offspring of aristocracy. . . He would sooner submit himself to a tax for paying for all the negroes in the United States, than saddle posterity with such a constitution. (p. 392.)

XXIX.

EXTRACTS FROM WILSON'S SPEECH BEFORE THE RATIFYING CONVENTION IN DEFENSE OF THE CONSTITUTION

(Bancroft, *History of The Constitution*, pp. 384-86.)

"The United States exhibit to the world the first instance of a nation unattacked by external force, unconvulsed by domestic insurrection, assembling voluntarily, deliberating fully, and deciding calmly that system of government under which they and their posterity should live. To form a good system of government for a single city or an inconsiderable state has been thought to require the strongest efforts of human genius; the views of the convention were expanded to a large portion of the globe.

"The difficulty of the business was equal to its magnitude. The United States contain already 13 governments mutually independent; their soil, climates, productions, dimensions and numbers are different; in many instances a difference and even an opposition subsists among their interests and is imagined to subsist in many more. Mutual concessions and sacrifices, the consequences of mutual forbearance and conciliation, were indispensably necessary to the success of the great work.

"The United States may adopt any one of four different systems. They may become consolidated into one government in which the separate existence of the states shall be entirely absolved. They may reject any plan of union, and act as unconnected states. They may form two or more confederacies. They may unite in one federal government republic. Neither of these systems found advocates in the late convention. The remaining system is a union in one confederate republic.

"The expanding quality of a government by which several states agree to become an assemblage of societies that constitute a new society, capable of increasing by means of further association, is peculiarly fitted for the United States. But this form of government left us almost without precedent or guide. Ancient history discloses, and barely discloses, to our view some confederate republics. The Swiss cantons are connected only by alliances; the United Netherlands constitute no new society; from the Germanic body little useful knowledge can be drawn.

"Since states as well as citizens are represented in the constitution before us, and form the objects on which that constitution is proposed to operate, it is necessary to mention a kind of liberty which has not yet received a name. I shall distinguish it by the name of federal liberty. The states should resign to the national government that part, and that part only, of their political liberty which, if placed in that government, will produce more good to the whole than if it had remained in the several states. While they resign this part of their political liberty, they retain the free and generous exercise of all their other faculties, so far as it is compatible with the welfare of the general and superintending confederacy.

"The powers of the federal government and those of the state governments are drawn from sources equally pure. The principle of representation, unknown to the ancients, is confined to a narrow corner of the British constitution. For the American states were reserved the glory and happiness of diffusing this vital principle throughout the constituent parts of government.

"The convention found themselves embarrassed with another difficulty of peculiar delicacy and importance; I mean that of drawing a proper line between the national government and the governments of the several states. Whatever object of government is confined in its operation and effects within the bounds of a particular state, should be considered as belonging to the government of that state; whatever object of govern- extends in its operation beyond the bounds of a particular state, should be considered as belonging to the government of the United States. To remove discretionary construction, the enumeration of particular instances in which the application of the principle ought to take place will be found to be safe, unexceptionable, and accurate.

"To control the power and conduct of the legislature by an overruling constitution, limiting and superintending the operations of legislative authority was an improvement in the science and practice of government reserved to the American state. Oft have I marked with silent pleasure and admiration the force and prevalence through the United States of the principle that the supreme power resides in the people, and that they will never part with it. There can be no disorder in the community but may here receive a radical cure. Error in the legislature may be corrected by the constitution; error in the constitution by the people. The streams of power run in different directions but they all originally flow from one abundant fountain. In this constitution all authority is derived from the people." (For entire speech *see* Elliot, *Debates*, v. 2, p. 418-34.)

Topics for Papers.

1 State briefly the difficulties enumerated in first two paragraphs, of making a new government.

2 What four forms of government were open to consideration? Is it true that the first three found no advocates?

3 What nations furnished examples according to Wilson? What other countries offered suggestion?

4 Explain the nature of "federal liberty."

5 State common source of federal and state governments. What is the vital principle in each?

6 What relations exist between the constitution, the people, and the government?

XXX.

PATRICK HENRY'S CHIEF OBJECTIONS TO THE CONSTITUTION

(Wirt, *Life of Patrick Henry*, p. 283.)

1 That it was a consolidated, instead of a confederated government; that in making it so, the delegates at Philadelphia had transcended the limits of their commission; changed fundamentally the relations which the states had chosen to bear to each other; annihilated their respective sovereignties; destroyed the barriers which divided them; and converted the whole into one solid empire. To this leading objection almost all the rest had reference, and were urged principally with the view to illustrate and enforce it.

2 The vast and alarming array of specific powers given to the general government and the wide

door opened for an unlimited extension of those powers, by the clause which authorized congress to pass all laws necessary to carry the given laws into effect. It was urged, that this clause rendered the previous specifications of powers an illusion ; since, by force of construction, congress might easily do anything and everything it chose.

3 The unlimited power of taxation of all kinds ; the states were no longer to be required, in their federative characters, to contribute their respective proportions towards the expenses and engagements of the general government ; but congress were authorized to go directly to the pockets of the people. . . . Such a power could not be exercised without just complaint. . . . The representatives in congress were too few to carry with them a knowledge of the wants and capacities of the people in the different parts of a large state. . . . Hence taxation ought to be left to the states themselves. . . . Mr. Henry said that he was willing to grant this power conditionally : i. e., upon the failure of the states to comply with requisitions from congress.

4 The power of raising armies, and building navies, and still more emphatically the control given to the general government over the militia of the states, was most strenuously opposed. . . . This republic should not be saddled with the expense of maintaining armies and navies . . .

to afford a pretext for increased taxes, and an augmented debt, and finally to subvert the liberties of her people.

5 The several clauses providing for the federal judiciary were objected to, on the ground of the clashing jurisdictions of the states and federal courts ; and secondly, because infinite power was given to congress to multiply inferior federal courts at pleasure.

6 It was contended that trial by jury was gone in civil cases, by that clause which gives to the supreme court appellate power over the law and the fact in every case. . . . In criminal cases also, the trial by jury was worse than gone, because it was admitted, that the common law would not be in force as to the federal courts.

7 The authority of the president to take command of the armies of the United States in person, was warmly resisted, on the ground that if he were a military character, he might easily convert them into an engine for the worst of purposes.

8 The cession of the whole treaty-making power to the president and senate was considered as one of the most formidable features in the instrument, inasmuch as it put it in the power of the president and any 10 senators, who might represent the five smallest states, to enter into the most ruinous foreign engagements.

9 The immense patronage of the president was objected to because it placed in his hands the

means of corrupting the congress, the navy and army, and of distributing throughout the society, a band of retainers in the shape of judges, revenue officers, and tax-gatherers.

10 It was insisted, that if we must adopt a constitution ceding away such vast powers, express and implied, and so fraught with danger to the liberties of the people, it ought at least to be guarded by a bill of rights.

Topics for Papers.

1 How many of the points in first paragraph are true, and how many are not true, as proven by experience ?

2 What checks upon an abuse by congress of its specific powers ?

3 How much truth in third paragraph ?

4 Judging from our navy and army in times of peace, have the people agreed with Henry ?

5 Has our country suffered from dangers recounted in paragraphs seven and eight ?

6 Explain how much of paragraph nine has come true.

XXXI.

EXTRACTS FROM IREDELL'S OBJECTIONS MADE IN NORTH CAROLINA CONVENTION AGAINST PUTTING A BILL OF RIGHTS IN THE CONSTITUTION

(Elliot, *Debates*, v. 4.)

"This is a subject of great consideration. It is a constitution which has been formed after much consideration and deliberation. It has the sanction of men of the first character for their probity and understanding. It has also had the solemn ratification of 10 states in the union. . . I readily confess my present opinion is strong in its favor. I have listened to every objection with attention but have not yet heard any that I thought would justify its rejection. . . . (p. 5.) This clause, vesting the power of impeachment in the house of representatives, is one of the greatest securities for due execution of all public offices. Every government requires it. Every man ought to be amenable for his conduct, and there are no persons so proper to complain of the public officers as the representatives of the people at large (p. 32.) . . Many are of the opinion that the power of the senate is too great; but I cannot think so, considering the great weight which the house of representatives will have. The house of representatives will be more numerous than the senate.

They will represent the immediate interests of the people. . . . There is always a danger of such a house becoming too powerful, and it is necessary to counteract its influence by giving great weight and authority to the other. (p. 38.)

. . . The manner in which our senate is to be chosen gives us an additional security. Our senators will not be chosen by a king, nor tainted by his influence. They are to be chosen by different legislatures in the union. . . . There is every probability that men elected in this manner will do their duty faithfully. . . . (p. 40.)

. . . "The only real security of liberty, in any country, is the jealousy and circumspection of the people themselves. Let them be watchful over their rulers. . . . That power which created the government can destroy it. Should this government, on trial, be found to want amendments, these amendments can be made in a regular method, in a mode prescribed by the constitution itself (p. 130.) . . . It is true that it would be very improper, if the senate had authority to prevent the house of representatives from protecting the people. It would be equally so, if the house of representatives were able to prevent the senate from protecting the sovereignty of the states. It is probable that either house would have sufficient authority to prevent much mischief. As to the suggestion of a tendency to aristocracy, it is totally groundless. . . . The president is only chosen for four years, liable to be impeached and dependent on the people at large for his re-election. Can this mode of appointment be said to have an aristocratical principle in it? The senate is chosen by the legislatures . . Will any man say that there are any aristocratical principles in a body who have no power independent of the people and whereof one third of the members are chosen every second year, by a wise and select body of electors? . . . (p. 133.)

"With regard to a bill of rights, this is a notion originating in England, where no written constitution is to be found, and the authority of their government is derived from the most remote antiquity. Magna charta is no constitution, but a solemn instrument ascertaining certain rights of individuals, by the legislature for the time being; and every article of which the legislature may at any time alter. . . . Had their constitution been fixed and certain, a bill of rights would have been useless, for the constitution would have shown plainly the extent of that authority which they were disputing about. Of what use, therefore, can a bill of rights be in this constitution, where the people expressly declare how much power they do give, and consequently retain all they do not give? . . . A bill of rights would not only be incongruous, but dangerous. No man could enumerate all the individual rights not relinquished by this constitution. . . . A bill of rights might operate as a snare rather than a protection. . . . Where there are powers of a particular nature and expressly defined, as in the case of the constitution before us, a bill of rights is unnecessary. . . (p. 149.)

"The trial by jury is different in different states. . . . Had it been inserted in the constitution, that the trial by jury should be as it had been heretofore, there would have been an example, for the first time in the world, of a judiciary belonging to the same government being different parts of the same country. . . The gentleman says that unalienable rights ought not to be given us. Those rights which are unalienable are not alienated. . . Let any one make what enumeration of rights he pleases, I will immediately mention 20 or 30 more rights not contained in it. . . If this constitution be adopted, it must be presumed the instrument will be in the hands of every man in America to see whether authority be usurped; and any person by inspecting it may see if the power claimed be enumerated."

Topics for Papers.

1 State briefly Iredell's argument in favor of the constitution.

2 What reasons for a bill of rights in the English constitution?

3 Why not a bill of rights in the American constitution?

Documents on the National Period

XXXII.

WASHINGTON'S PROCLAMATION OF NEUTRALITY

(Sparks, *Writings of George Washington*, v. 10, p. 535.)

"Whereas it appears that a state of war exists between Austria, Prussia, Sardinia, Great Britain, and the United Netherlands, on the one part, and France on the other; and the duty and interest of the United States require that they should with sincerity and good faith adopt and pursue a conduct friendly and impartial towards the belligerent powers;

"I have therefore thought fit by these presents to declare the disposition of the United States to observe the conduct aforesaid towards those powers respectively, and to exhort and warn the citizens of the United States carefully to avoid all acts and proceedings whatsoever, which may in any manner tend to contravene such disposition.

"And I do hereby also make known that whosoever of the citizens of the United States shall render himself liable to punishment or forfeiture under the law of nations, by committing, aiding, or abetting hostilities against any of the said powers, or by carrying to any of them those articles which are deemed contraband by the modern usage of nations, will not receive the protection of the United States against such punishment or forfeiture; and further, that I have given instructions to those officers, to whom it belongs, to cause prosecutions to be instituted against all persons, who shall within the cognizance of the courts of the United States, violate the law of nations with respect to the powers at war, or any of them." . . .

Topics for Papers.

1 What war is alluded to in the proclamation? Why did Americans take an unusual interest in it?

2 State cause and purpose of the proclamation.

3 What line of conduct is marked out for the people of the United States? Has this grown into a custom or not?

4 What is meant by the law of nations? By contraband articles?

5 What is the general significance of the proclamation?

XXXIII.

EXTRACTS FROM KENTUCKY AND VIRGINIA RESOLUTIONS

(Elliot, *Debates*, v. 4. pp. 540–545.)

"Resolved, That this assembly doth emphatically and peremptorily declare, that it views the powers of the federal government as resulting from the compact to which the states are parties, as limited by the plain sense and intention of the instrument constituting that compact, as no further valid than they are authorized by the grants enumerated in that compact; and that in case of a deliberate, palpable and dangerous exercise of other powers, not granted by said compact, the states who are parties thereto, have the right, and are in duty bound, to interpose for arresting the progress of the evil and for maintaining within their respective limits the authorities, rights and liberties, appertaining to them." (Va.)

"Resolved, . . . that whenever the general government assumes undelegated powers, its acts are unauthoritative, void, and of no force; that to this compact each state acceded as a state, and is an integral party; that this government, created by this compact, was not made the exclusive or final judge of the extent of the powers delegated to itself, since that would have made its discretion, and not the constitution, the measure of its powers ; but that, as in all other cases of compact among parties having no common judge, each party has an equal right to judge for itself, as well of infractions as the mode and measure of redress." (Ky. 1798.)

"Resolved, That . . . the several states who formed that instrument being sovereign and independent, have the unquestionable right to judge of the infraction ; and that a nullification by those sovereignties, of all unauthorized acts done under color of that instrument, is the right ful remedy." (Ky. 1799.)

Topics for Papers.

1 According to above resolutions indicate
- *a* Nature of the organization established by the constitution.
- *b* Extent of powers granted to the general government.
- *c* Who is judge of violations of the constitution.
- *d* Remedy for unconstitutional acts.

2 Which of these doctrines are now held true? What inferences ?

XXXIV.

JEFFERSON'S FIRST INAUGURAL

(Jefferson, *Writings,* v. 8, pp. 1–6.)

"During the contest of opinion through which we have passed, the animation of discussion and of exertions has sometimes worn an aspect which might impose on strangers unused to think freely and to speak and to write what they think; but this being now decided by the voice of the nation, . . . all will, of course, arrange themselves under the will of the law, and unite in common efforts for the common good. All, too, will bear in mind this sacred principle, that though the will of the majority is in all cases to prevail, that will, to be rightful, must be reasonable; that the minority possess their equal rights, which equal laws must protect, and to violate which would be oppression. Let us, then, fellow-citizens, unite with one heart and one mind. . . But every difference of opinion is not a difference of principle. We have called by different names brethren of the same principle. We are all republicans—we are federalists. If there be any among us who would wish to dissolve this union or to change its republican form, let them stand undisturbed as monuments of the safety with which error of opinion may be tolerated where reason is left free to combat it. . .

I believe this, on the contrary, the strongest government on earth. I believe it is the only one where every man, at the call of the laws, would fly to the standard of the law and would meet invasions of the public order as his own personal concern. . . Still one thing more, fellow-citizens, a wise and frugal government, which shall restrain men from injuring one another, which shall leave them otherwise free to regulate their own pursuits of industry and improvement, and shall not take from the mouth of labor the bread it has earned. This is the sum of good government and this is necessary to close the circle of our felicities. . . It is proper that you should understand what I deem the essential principles of our government. . . Equal and exact justice to all men, of whatever state or persuasion, religious or political; peace, commerce, and honest friendship, with all nations—entangling alliances with none; the support of the state governments in all their rights, as the most competent administrations for our domestic concerns and the surest bulwarks against anti-republican tendencies; the preservation of the general government in its whole constitutional vigor, as the sheet anchor of our peace at home and safety abroad. . . The supremacy of the civil over the military authority; economy in the public expense, that labor may be lightly burdened; the honest payment of our debts and sacred preservation of the public faith."

Topics for Papers.

1 Rights of the minority.
  a Enumerate these rights as found in the above.
  b To what particular minority if any, did he refer ?
  c What other expressions show Jefferson's desire to make friends with the minority ?

2 Good government.
  a What constitutes the sum of good government ?
  b Enumerate what Jefferson regarded as the principles of our government.
  c Are these all still regarded as sound doctrines ?

XXXV.

HOW THE WAR OF 1812 NATIONALIZED SENTIMENT

(Schurz's Clay, v. 1, pp. 64–65 ; 134.)

Henry Clay in 1811.

"What is the nature of this government ? It is emphatically federal, vested with an aggregate of specified powers for general purposes conceded by existing sovereignties, who have themselves retained what is not so conceded. It is said there are cases in which it must act on implied powers. This is not controverted, but the implication must be necessary and *obviously* flow from the enumerated power with which it is allied. . . In all cases where incidental powers are acted upon, the principal and the incidental ought to be congenial. . . and partake of a common nature. The incidental power ought to be strictly subordinate and limited to the end proposed to be attained by the specific power. In other words, under the name of accomplishing our object which is specified, the power implied ought not to be made to embrace other objects which are not specified in the constitution."

Henry Clay in 1816.

"The constitution contains powers delegated and prohibitory, powers expressed and powers constructive. It vests in congress all powers necessary to give effect to the enumerated powers.

The powers that may be so necessary are deducible by construction. They are not defined in the constitution. They are in their nature undefinable. With regard to the degree of necessity, various rules have been, at different times, laid down ; but perhaps, at last, there is no other than a sound and honest judgment, exercised under the control which belongs to the constitution and the people. It is manifest that this necessity may not be perceived at one time under one state of things. The constitution, it is true, never changes; it is always the same; but the force of circumstances and the lights of experience may evolve, to the fallible persons charged with its administration, the fitness and necessity of a particular exercise of constructive power to-day, which they did not see at a former period."

Topics for Papers.

1 State the points of resemblance between the doctrines of the first extract given above and the doctrines of the Kentucky and Virginia Resolutions.

2 Compare and contrast the two extracts as to their political doctrines.

3 Draw conclusions based on this comparison and contrast.

XXXVI.

THE HARTFORD CONVENTION

(Niles' Weekly Register, v. 7, pp. 308–313.)

Nature of the Government:

That the acts of congress in violation of the constitution are absolutely void, is an undeniable position. It does not, however, consist with the respect and forbearance due from a confederate state towards the general government to fly to open resistance upon every infraction of the constitution. The mode and energy of the opposition should always conform to the nature of the violation, the intention of the authors, and the extent of the injury inflicted ; the determination manifested to persist in it, and the danger of delay. But in cases of deliberate, dangerous and palpable infractions of the constitution affecting the sovereignty of a state and liberties of the people, it is not only the right but the duty of such a state, to interpose its authority for their protection in the manner best calculated to secure that end. When emergencies occur, which are beyond the reach of the judicial tribunals, or too pressing to admit of the delay incident to their forms, states, which have no common umpire, must be their own judges, and execute their own decisions. It will thus be proper for the several states to await the obnoxious measures recommended by the Secretary of War, or pending before congress, and to use their power according to the character these measures shall finally assume, as effectually to protect their own sovereignty, and the rights and liberties of their citizens.

Amendments to the Constitution :

Resolved, that the following amendments of the constitution of the United States be recommended to the states represented as aforesaid . . . that the said states shall persevere . . . until the same shall be effected.

First. Representatives and direct taxes shall be appointed among the several states . . . according to their respective numbers of free persons. . . .

Second. No new state shall be admitted into the union by congress . . . without the concurrence of two-thirds of both houses.

Third. Congress shall not have power to lay an embargo . . . for more than sixty days.

Fourth. Congress shall not have power without the concurrence of two-thirds of both houses, to interdict the commercial intercourse between the United States and any foreign nation. . . .

Fifth. Congress shall not make nor declare war . . . without the concurrence of two-thirds of both houses. . . .

Sixth. No person who shall hereafter be naturalized shall be eligible as a member of the senate or house of representatives of the United States, nor capable of holding any civil office under the authority of the United States.

Seventh. The same person shall not be elected president of the United States a second time; nor shall the president be elected from the same state two terms in succession.

Suggestions for Study.

1 State the points of agreement with the Kentucky and Virginia Resolutions and draw conclusions.

2 Contrast with Kentucky and Virginia Resolutions as to their origin and effects.

3 Account for the difference in their effects.

4 Which of these amendments had been discussed before? Which since?

XXXVII.

THE MONROE DOCTRINE

(Monroe's Message, Dec. 2, 1823. Annals of Congress; 18th Congress.)

". . . . In the wars of the European powers, in matters relating to themselves, we have never taken any part, nor does it comport with our policy so to do. It is only when our rights are invaded or seriously menaced, that we resent injuries or make preparation for defense. With the movements in this hemisphere we are of necessity more immediately connected, and by causes which must be obvious to all enlightened and impartial observers. The political system of the allied powers is essentially different in this respect from that of America. This difference proceeds from that which exists in their respective governments. And to the defense of our own, which has been achieved by the loss of so much blood and treasure, and matured by the wisdom of their most enlightened citizens, and under which we have enjoyed unexampled felicity, this whole nation is devoted. We owe it, therefore, to candor, and to the amicable relations existing between the United States and those powers to declare, that we should consider any attempt on their part to extend their system to any portion of this hemisphere as dangerous to our peace and safety. With the existing colonies or dependencies of any European power we have not interfered, and shall not interfere. But with the governments who have declared their independence, and maintained it, and whose independence we have, on great consideration, and on just principles, acknowledged, we could not view any interposition for the purpose of oppressing them, or controlling in any other manner their destiny, by any European power, in any other light than as the manifestation of an unfriendly disposition towards the United States. . . .

"Our policy in regard to Europe, which was adopted at an early stage of the wars which have so long agitated that quarter of the globe, nevertheless remains the same, which is, not to interfere in the internal concerns of any of its powers; . . . to cultivate friendly relations with it, and to preserve those relations by a frank, firm, and manly policy; meeting, in all instances, the just claims of every power, submitting to injuries from none. But in regard to these continents, circumstances are eminently and conspicuously different. It is impossible that the allied powers should extend their political system to any portion of either continent without endangering our peace and happiness; nor can any one believe that our southern brethren, if left to themselves, would adopt it of their own accord. It is equally impossible, therefore, that we should behold such interposition, in any form, with indifference." . . .

Topics for Papers

1 When did the policy stated in the first paragraph originate?

2 Quote that part of the message which states the Monroe doctrine.

3 What was the policy of our government toward the other American governments?

4 Why would it endanger our peace for European powers to extend their political system to America?

5 Do Americans believe in this doctrine yet? Prove your answer.

XXXVIII.

JACKSON'S PROCLAMATION AGAINST NULLIFICATION

(Elliot, *Debates*, v. 4, p. 582.)

"And whereas the said ordinance prescribes to the people of South Carolina a course of conduct in direct violation of their duty as citizens of the United States, contrary to the laws of their country, subversive of its constitution, and having for its object the destruction of the union . . . that union which, coeval with our political existence, led our fathers, without any other ties to unite them than those of patriotism and a common cause, through a sanguinary struggle to a glorious independence—that sacred union hitherto inviolate, which, perfected by our happy constitution, has brought us, by the favor of heaven, to a state of prosperity at home, and a high consideration abroad, rarely, if ever, equaled in the history of nations; to preserve this bond of our political existence from destruction, to maintain inviolate this state of national honor and prosperity, and to justify the confidence my fellow-citizens have reposed in me, I, Andrew Jackson, President of the United States, have thought proper to issue this, my proclamation, stating my views of the constitution and laws applicable to the measures adopted by the convention of South Carolina and to the reasons they have put forth to sustain them, declaring the course which duty will require me to pursue, and, appealing to the understanding and patriotism of the people, warn them of the consequences that must inevitably result from an observance of the dictates of the convention." . . .

"The ordinance is founded, not on the indefeasible right of resisting acts which are plainly unconstitutional and too oppressive to be endured, but on the strange position that any one state may not only declare an act of congress void, but prohibit its execution ; that they may do this consistently with the constitution; that the true construction of that instrument permits a state to retain its place in the union, and yet be bound by no other of its laws than those it may choose to consider as constitutional." . . .

"But reasoning on this subject is superfluous, when our social compact, in express terms, declares that the laws of the United States, its constitution, and treaties made under it, are the supreme law of the land ; and, for greater caution, adds that the judges in every state shall be bound thereby, anything in the constitution or laws of any state to the contrary notwithstanding. And it may be asserted without fear of refutation, that no federative government could exist without a similar provision." . . . "The constitution of the United States, then, forms a government, not a league ; and whether it be formed by compact between the states, or in any other manner, its character is the same. It is a government in which all the people are represented, which operates directly on the people individually, not upon the states . . . they retained all the power they did not grant. But each state having expressly parted with so many powers as to constitute, jointly with the other states, a single nation, cannot, from that period, possess any right to secede, because such secession does not break a league, but destroys the unity of a nation; and any injury to that unity is not only a breach which would result from the contravention of a compact, but it is an offense against the whole union. To say that any state may at pleasure secede from the union, is to say that the United States are not a nation; because it would be a solecism to contend that any part of a nation might dissolve its connection with the other parts, to their injury or ruin, without committing any offense."

Topics for Papers.

1 What was the purpose of the ordinance of nullification according to its authors? According to Jackson?

2 State fundamental purpose of the proclamation?

3 Ordinance based on erroneous doctrines.

a What would be true grounds for resistance?

b What is the ground for this ordinance?

c Does this ordinance resemble or differ from Kentucky and Virginia resolutions?

4 Does Jackson interpret the constitution correctly?

5 State how Jackson's view of nature of the

government differs from that asserted in Kentucky and Virginia resolutions.

6 How do you account for such radically different views of members of the same party?

XXXIX.

AGITATION FOR SLAVERY RESTRICTION

The New York Assembly (1820): Whereas, the inhibiting the further extension of slavery in these United States is a subject of deep concern among the people of this state; and whereas we consider slavery as an evil much to be deplored; and that every constitutional barrier should be interposed to prevent its further extension; and the constitution of the United States clearly gives congress the right to require of new states, not comprised within the original boundaries of the United States, the prohibition of slavery, as a condition of admission. . . .

The New Jersey Legislature (1820): . . . That the further admission of territories into this union, without restriction of slavery, would, in their opinion, essentially impair the right of this and other existing states to equal representation in congress . . . That inasmuch as congress have a clear right to refuse the admission of a territory into the union . . . they ought in the present case to exercise their absolute discretion in order to preserve the political rights of the several existing states, and prevent the great national disgrace and multiplied mischiefs. . . .

The Legislature of Pennsylvania (1819): . . . That the senators of this state . . . are hereby instructed and that the representatives . . . are hereby requested, to vote against the admission of any territory as a state into the union unless said territory shall stipulate and agree that the further introduction of slavery . . . shall be prohibited.

Legislature of Delaware (1820): . . . That it is, in the opinion of this General Assembly, the constitutional right of the United States, in congress assembled, to enact and establish, as one of the conditions for the admission of a new state into the union a provision which shall effectually prevent the further introduction of slavery into such state; and that a true regard for the interests of such state, as well as of the other states, require that the same shall be done. . . .

The Ohio Legislature (1820): Whereas, the existence of slavery in our country has ever been deemed a great moral and political evil, and its tendency directly calculated to impair our national character, and materially affecting our national happiness, and inasmuch as the extension of a slave population in the United States is fraught with the most fearful consequences to the permanency and durability of our republican institutions . . . resolved . . . that our senators and representatives in congress be requested to use their zealous endeavors to prevent the adoption of so odious and dangerous a measure. . . .

The Wilmot Proviso (1846): Provided, that as an express and fundamental condition to the acquisition of any territory from the republic of Mexico by the United States, by virtue of any treaty which may be negotiated between them, and to the use by the executive of the moneys herein appropriated, neither slavery nor involuntary servitude shall ever exist in any part of said territory. . . .

XL.

EXTRACTS FROM THE FREE SOIL PLATFORM, 1848

(Political Text-Book for 1860.)

That we, the people here assembled, remembering the example of our fathers, in the days of the first declaration of independence, putting our trust in God for the triumph of our cause, and invoking His guidance in our endeavors to advance it, do now plant ourselves upon the national platform of freedom in opposition to the sectional platform of slavery.

That slavery in the several states of this union

which recognize its existence, depends upon state laws alone, which cannot be repealed or be modified by the federal government, and for which laws that government is not responsible. We therefore propose no interference by congress with slavery within the limits of any state.

That the true, and in the judgment of this convention, the only safe means of preventing the extension of slavery into territory now free, is to prohibit its extension in all such territory by an act of congress.

That we accept the issue which the slave power has forced upon us, and to their demand for more slave states, and more slave territory, our calm but final answer is, no more slave states and no more slave territory.

That we inscribe on our own banner, "Free soil, free speech, free labor, and free men," and under it we will fight on and fight ever until a triumphant victory shall reward our exertions.

Topics for Papers

1 Why do they refer to declaration of independence?

2 What conclusion was drawn from the fact that slavery was a state institution?

3 How could congress, with no power over it in the states, prohibit slavery in the territories?

4 When did the north begin to demand con-

gressional prohibition of slavery in the territories?

5 Why could slavery not accept this position right or wrong?

6 State the issue attaching to each of the quoted phrases in last paragraph.

XLI.

HENRY CLAY ON THE COMPROMISE OF 1850

(Political Text-Book for 1860, p. 77.)

"I am extremely sorry to hear the senator from Mississippi say that he requires, first, the extension of the Missouri compromise line to the Pacific, and also that he is not satisfied with that, but requires, if I understood him correctly, a positive provision for the admission of slavery south of that line. And now, Sir, coming from a slave state, as I do, I owe it to myself, I owe it to truth, I owe it to the subject to state that no earthly power could induce me to vote for a specific measure for the introduction of slavery where it had not before existed, either south or north of that line. Coming as I do from a slave state, it is my solemn, deliberate and well-matured determination that no power, no earthly power, shall compel me to vote for the positive introduction of slavery either south or north of that line. Sir, while you reproach, and justly too, our British ancestors for the introduction of this institution upon the continent of America I am, for one, unwilling that the posterity of the present inhabitants of California and New Mexico, shall reproach us for doing just what we reproach Great Britain for doing to us. If the citizens of those territories choose to establish slavery, I am for admitting them with such provisions in their constitutions; but then it will be their own work, and not ours, and their posterity will have to reproach them, and not us, for forming constitutions allowing the institution of slavery to exist among them. These are my views, Sir, and I choose to express them; and I care not how extensively and universally they are known. . . . I am willing to stand aside and make no legislative enactment one way or the other—to lay off the territories without the Wilmot Proviso, on the one hand, with which I understand we are threatened, or without an attempt to introduce a clause for the introduction of slavery into the territories."

Suggestions for Study.

1 Was Henry Clay an anti-slavery man? Give proofs.

2 Did Free-soil men agree with this speech? Why?

3 What principle guided Clay in the above discussion?

4 What two extremes did he avoid by this plan of organizing the territories?

XLII.

THE IRREPRESSIBLE CONFLICT

Lincoln before the Illinois Republican State Convention June 16, 1858:—

"If we could first know where we are, and whither we are tending, we could better judge what to do, and how to do it. We are now far into the fifth year since a policy was initiated with the avowed object and confident promise of putting an end to slavery agitation. Under the operation of that policy that agitation has not only not ceased but has constantly augmented. In my opinion it will not cease until a crisis shall have been reached and passed. "A house divided against itself cannot stand." I believe this government cannot endure permanently half slave and half free. I do not expect the union to be dissolved—I do not expect the house to fall—but I do expect it will cease to be divided. It will become all one thing or all the other. Either the opponents of slavery will arrest the further spread of it, and place it where the public mind shall rest in the belief that it is in the course of ultimate extinction; or its advocates will push it forward till it shall become alike lawful in all the states, old as well as new, North as well as South."—Works of Lincoln, vol. 1, p. 240.

Seward at Rochester, N. Y., Oct 25, 1858:—

". . . But in another aspect the United States constitute only one nation. Increase of population, which is filling the states out to their very borders, together with a new and extended network of railroads and other avenues, and an internal commerce which daily becomes more intimate, is rapidly bringing the states into a higher and more perfect social unity or consolidation. Thus, these antagonistic systems are continually coming into closer contact, and collision results.

"Shall I tell you what this collision means? They who think that it is accidental, unnecessary, the work of interested, or fanatical agitators, and therefore ephemeral, mistake these altogether. It is an irrepressible conflict between opposing and enduring forces, and it means that the United States must and will, sooner or later, become either entirely a slaveholding nation, or a free-labor nation. Either the cotton and rice fields of South Carolina, and the sugar plantations of Louisiana will ultimately be tilled by free-labor . . . or else the rye-fields and wheat-fields of Massachusetts and New York must again be surrendered by their farmers to slave culture. . . It is the failure to apprehend this great truth that induces so many unsuccessful attempts at final compromise between the slave and the free states. . . .

"I know and you know that a revolution has begun. I know and all the world knows that revolutions never go backwards. Twenty senators and a hundred representatives proclaim boldly in congress to-day sentiments and opinions and principles of freedom which hardly so many men, even in this free state, dared to utter in their own homes twenty years ago."

Suggestions for study.

1 To what policy does Lincoln refer in his second sentence? Is his statement of its purpose and result true? Prove.

2 Does the conflict seem an irrepressible one to Lincoln? Prove.

3 What fundamental cause does Seward find for this conflict?

4 Name the points of agreement between the two extracts.

5 Why did men compromise, and why did compromises fail?

XLIII.

EXTRACTS FROM THE LINCOLN–DOUGLAS DEBATES

(Complete Works of Lincoln, v. 1, pp. 308, 315.)

Lincoln's Questions to Douglas:

"1 If the people of Kansas shall, by means entirely unobjectionable in all other respects, adopt a state constitution, and ask admission into the union under it, before they have the requisite number of inhabitants according to the English bill,—some ninety-three thousand,—will you vote to admit them?

"2 Can the people of a United States territory, in any lawful way, against the wish of any citizen of the United States, exclude slavery from its limits prior to the formation of a state constitution?

"3 If the Supreme Court of the United States shall decide that states cannot exclude slavery from their limits, are you in favor of acquiescing in, adopting and following such decision, as a rule of action?

"4 Are you in favor of acquiring additional territory, in disregard of how such acquisition may affect the nation on the slavery question?"

Douglas's answer to the second question.

. . . "I answer emphatically . . . that, in my

opinion, the people of a territory can, by lawful means, exclude slavery from their limits prior to the formation of a state constitution. . . . It matters not what way the Supreme Court may hereafter decide as to the abstract question, whether slavery may or may not go into a territory under the constitution, the people have the lawful means to introduce it or exclude it as they please, for the reason that slavery cannot exist a day or an hour anywhere unless it is supported by local police regulations. Those police regulations can only be established by the local legislature, and if the people are opposed to slavery they will elect representatives to that body who will, by unfriendly legislation, effectually prevent the introduction of it into their midst. If, on the contrary, they are for it, their legislation will favor its extension."

Topics for Papers.

1 What were some of the questions before the people in 1858?

2–Show the relation between Lincoln's second question and the Dred Scott Decision.

3-In what dilemma did the second question place Douglas? Explain.

4 State the effects of Douglas's answer:

a–On the canvass for the senatorship

b–On the slaveholders.

XLIV.

SENTIMENTS FROM THE CHARLESTON CONVENTION

(Political Text-Book for 1860.)

Mr. Avery *of North Carolina*—I have stated that we demand at the hands of our northern brethren . . . that the great principle which we cherish should be recognized, and . . . I speak the common sentiments of our constituents at home; and I intend no reflection upon those who entertain a different opinion, when I say that the results and ultimate consequences to the southern states of this confederacy, if the popular sovereignty doctrine be adopted as the doctrine of the democratic party, would be as dangerous and subversive of their rights as the adoption of the principle of congressional intervention or prohibition. We say that, in a contest for the occupation of the territories of the United States, the southern men encumbered with slaves cannot compete with the emigrant aid society at the north. We say that the emigrant aid society can send a voter to one of the territories of the United States, to determine a question relating to slavery, for the sum of $200, while it would cost the southern man the sum of $1500. . . .

Let us make a platform about which there can be no doubt, so that every man, north and south, may stand side by side on all issues connected with slavery. . . . All we demand at your hands is, that there shall be no equivocation and no doubt in the popular mind as to what our principles are.

MR. MOUTON *of Louisiana*—Are we not divided, and divided in such a manner that we can never be reconciled, because we are divided upon principle? Can we agree to the platform adopted by the majority of the convention, and then go home to our constituents and put one construction on it, while northern democrats put another? No, Mr. President, I think I speak the sentiment of my state when I say that she will never play such a part (cheers). If we are to fight the black republicans together, let us do it with a bold front; let us use the same arms; let us sustain the same principles.

MR. MILTON *of Florida*—Since that time, gentlemen, according to your own report, a mighty power has arisen in your midst, deriving much of its strength and support from the democrats of the north. I allude to the black republican party, a party which promulgates to the country that they have a higher law, a law known only to themselves, . . . but superior to the constitution.

MR. BRYAN *of Texas* (who was received with

loud cheers)—Mr. President and gentlemen of the convention: Texas, through her delegates on this floor, on the land of Calhoun, where "truth, justice and the constitution," was proclaimed to the south, says to the south, this day you stand erect (loud cheers). Whilst we deprecate the necessity which calls for our parting with the delegates from the other states of this confederacy, yet it is an event that we, personally, have long looked to. Educated in a northern college, I there first learned that there was a north and a south; there were two literary societies, one northern and the other southern. In the churches, the Methodist church, the Baptist church, the Presbyterian church, are north and south. Gentlemen of the north and northwest, God grant that there may be but one democratic party.

MR. GAULDEN *of Georgia*—I am an African slave-trader. I am one of those southern men who believe that slavery is right, morally, religiously, socially and politically (applause). I believe that the institution of slavery has done more for this country, more for civilization, than all other interests put together. I believe if it were in the power of this country to strike down the institution of slavery, it would put civilization back 200 years. . . . I believe that the general government by the constitution never had any right to legislate upon this subject. I believe that our government was a confederation of states for certain specified objects with limited powers ; that the domestic relations of each state are to be and should be left to themselves ; that this eternal slavery question has been the bone of contention between the north and south, which if kept in the halls of congress must break up this government. I am one of those who believe in non-intervention, either in the states or the territories (applause). I am not in favor of breaking up this government upon an impracticable issue, upon a mere theory. I believe that this doctrine of protection to slavery in the territories is a mere theory, a mere abstraction (applause). Practically it can be of no consequence to the south, for the reason that the infant has been strangled before it was born (laughter). You have cut off the supply of slaves ; you have crippled the institution of slavery in the states by your unjust laws, and it is mere folly and madness now to ask for protection for a nonentity, for a thing which is not there. . . . We can never make another slave state with our present supply of slaves. . . . If you make another slave state from our new territories with the present supply of slaves you will be obliged to give up another state, either Maryland, Delaware, or Virginia, to free soil upon the north. . . . We, the democracy of the south, are mere carpet knights. It is no trouble for us to be democrats (applause and laughter). When I look to the northern democrats, I see them standing up there and breasting the tide of fanaticism, oppression, wrong, and slander, with which they have to contend. I view in these men types of the old ancient Romans ; I view in them all that is patriotic and noble ; and, for one, I am not willing to cut loose from them (great cheering). . . . I am not willing to disintegrate, dismember, and turn them over to the ruthless hands of the thieving black republicans of the north.

Topics.

1 To what great principle does Mr. Avery refer ?

2 Prove that popular sovereignty was dangerous to the south.

3 Why did it cost the south more than the north to send emigrants to Kansas ?

4 What is the meaning of Bryan's speech ?

5 Why did Gaulden please the convention ?

XLV.

EXTRACTS SHOWING THE GROWTH OF A CONSPIRACY

(Nicolay and Hay's Abraham Lincoln, v. 2, pp. 300–326.)

"He (Gov. Wise) says the governors of N. C., S. C., and La., have already agreed to rendezvous at Raleigh . . . He says, further, that he had officially requested you to exchange with Virginia . . . percussion for flint muskets. . . . Virginia probably has more arms than the other southern states, and would divide in case of need. In a letter yesterday to a committee in South Carolina, I give it as my judgment, in case of Fremont's election, the south should not pause, but proceed at once to immediate, absolute, and eternal separation."—*J. M. Mason,* Senator from Virginia to Jefferson Davis, Secretary of War, Sept. 30, 1856.

"But if we could do as our fathers did—organize committees of safety all over the cotton states . . . we shall fire the southern heart and instruct the southern mind . . . and, at the proper moment, by one organized concerted action we can precipitate the cotton states into revolution."—*Wm. L. Yancy,* Ala., June, 1858.

"The objects of the association are :

"First. To conduct a correspondence with leading men in the south, and by an interchange of information and views prepare the slave states to meet the impending crisis.

"Second. To prepare, print, and distribute in the slave states, tracts, pamphlets, etc., designed to awaken them to a conviction of their danger, and to urge the necessity of resisting Northern and Federal aggression.

"Third. To inquire into the defenses of the state,

and to collect and arrange information which may aid the legislature to establish promptly an efficient military organization."—*Robert N. Gourdin*, Chairman Executive Committee of "The 1860 Association," Nov. 19, 1860.

"While engaged in consultation with the governor (of Miss.) . . . a telegraphic message was handed me from two members of Mr. Buchanan's cabinet. . . My presence there was desired on account of the influence . . . I might exercise with the president. . . On paying my respects to the president, he told me that he had finished the rough draft of his message, but that it was still open to revision and amendment, and that he would like to read it to me. He did so and very kindly accepted all the modifications which I suggested. The message was, however, afterwards somewhat changed."—*Jefferson Davis*, Nov. 1860.

"I think it likely that the president will state forcibly what he considers the grievances of the south, that he will add that he does not think . . . it wise policy for the state to adopt (secession) . . . As long as Cobb and Thompson retain seats in the cabinet, you may feel confident that no action has been taken which seriously affects the position of any southern state."—*W. H. Trescott*, Assistant Secretary of State, to T. F. Drayton, Nov. 19, 1860.

"I arrived here . . . from New York where I had gone at the suggestion of Mr. Floyd to engage Mr. G. B. Lamar, president of the Bank of the Republic, to make an offer to the secretary for such a number of muskets as we might require . . . and to-day the secretary has written to the commanding officer [at] Watervliet arsenal to deliver five or ten thousand muskets . . . to Mr. Lamar's order. . . I am very anxious to get possession of the arms . . . and forward them to Charleston."—*T. F. Drayton* to Gov. Gist of S. C., Washington, Nov. 23, 1860.

Topics.

1 Make a list of persons named and of their official positions.

2 State briefly what each was trying to do.

3 Draw conclusions from above extracts.

XLVI.

THE CAUSE AND MOTIVE OF SECESSION

(From Nicolay and Hay's Lincoln, v. 2, pp. 408--409.)

"They (the border states) say that we have no right to take them out of the union against their will. I want to know what right they have to keep us in the union against our will. If we want to go out let us go. If they want to stay let them stay. They are sovereign and independent states, and have a right to decide these questions. . . . I am satisfied, however, that they will go, when the time comes for them to decide. But, sir, they complain of us that we make so much noise and confusion on the subject of fugitive slaves when we are not affected by the vitiated public sentiment of the northern states. . . . I know that we do not suffer in this respect; it is not the want of good faith in the northern people, so far as the reclamation of fugitive slaves is concerned, that is causing the southern states around the Gulf of Mexico and the Southern Atlantic coast to move in this great revolution. . . . Sir, we look infinitely beyond this petty loss of a few negroes. We know what is coming in this union. It is universal emancipation. . . . We intend to avoid it if we can."—*Senator Iverson*, of Georgia, in the Senate, Dec., 1860.)

"Our position is thoroughly identified with the institution of slavery—the greatest material interest in the world. . . . A blow at slavery is a blow at commerce and civilization. That blow has long been aimed at the institution, and was at the point of reaching its consummation. There was no choice left us but submission to the mandates of abolition, or a dissolution of the union, whose principles had been subverted to work out our ruin. We must either submit to degradation, and loss of property worth four billions of money, or we must secede from the union."—(Mississippi Secession Convention, Jan. 1861.)

"The prevailing ideas entertained by him (Jefferson) and most of the leading statesmen at the time of the formation of the old constitution, were that the enslavement of the African was in violation of the laws of nature; that it was wrong in *principle*, socially, morally, and politically. . . . Our new government is founded upon exactly the opposite idea; its foundations are laid, its corner-stone rests upon the great truth that the negro is not the equal of the white man. . . . This, our new government, is the first, in the history of the world, based upon this great physical, philosophical and moral truth. . . . This stone which was rejected by the first builders 'is become the chief of the corner'—the real corner-stone—in our new edifice."—*Vice-President Stephens* at Savannah, 1861.

Suggestions for Study.

1 What motive for secession seemed uppermost in the southern mind?

2 Are any other causes given?

3 Search for a cause or motive not connected with slavery.

4 What inferences do you draw from your search?

XLVII.

LINCOLN'S FIRST INAUGURAL

(Works of Lincoln, v. 2, p. 1–7.)

"Fellow-citizens of the United States: In compliance with a custom as old as the government itself, I appear before you to address you briefly, and to take in your presence the oath prescribed by the constitution of the United States, to be taken by the president before he enters upon the execution of his office. . .

"Apprehension seems to exist among the people of the southern states, that by the accession of a republican administration, their property and their peace and their personal security are to be endangered. There has never been any reasonable cause for such apprehension. Indeed, the most ample evidence to the contrary has all the while existed and been open to their inspection. It is found in nearly all the published speeches of him who now addresses you. I do but quote from one of those speeches when I declare that I have no purpose, directly or indirectly, to interfere with the institution of slavery, in the states where it exists. I believe I have no lawful right to do so, and I have no inclination to do so. Those who nominated and elected me, did so with a full knowledge that I had made this and many similar declarations and had never recanted them. . .

"I now reiterate these sentiments, and in doing so, I only press upon the public attention the most conclusive evidence of which the case is susceptible, that the property, peace and security of no section, are to be in any wise endangered by the new incoming administration. . . I hold, that in contemplation of universal law, and of the constitution, the union of the states is perpetual. . . In doing this there need be no bloodshed or violence; and there shall be none, unless it be forced upon the national authority. The power confided to me will be used to hold, occupy and possess the property and places belonging to the government and to collect the duties and imposts; but beyond what may be necessary for these objects, there will be no invasion, no using of force against or among the people anywhere. Where hostility to the United States, in any interior locality shall be so great and universal as to prevent competent resident citizens from holding the federal offices, there will be no attempt to force obnoxious strangers among the people for that object. While the strict legal right may exist in the government, to enforce the exercise of these offices, the attempt to do so would be so irritating, and so nearly impracticable, withal, that I deem it better to forego, for the time, the use of such offices. . .

"Physically speaking, we cannot separate. We cannot remove our respective sections from each other, nor build an impassable wall between them. A husband and wife may be divorced, and go out of the presence, and beyond the reach of each other, but the different parts of our country cannot do this. . .

"This country, with its institutions, belongs to the people who inhabit it. Whenever they shall grow weary of the existing government, they can exercise the constitutional right of amending it, or their revolutionary right to dismember or overthrow it. I cannot be ignorant of the fact that many worthy and patriotic citizens are desirous of having the national constitution amended. . .

"My countrymen, one and all, think calmly and well upon this whole subject. Nothing valuable can be lost by taking time. If there be an object to hurry any of you in hot haste to a step which you would never take deliberately, that object will be frustrated by taking time. Such of you as are now dissatisfied, still have the old constitution unimpaired, and on the sensitive point, the laws of your own framing under it; while the new administration will have no immediate power, if it would, to change either. If it were admitted that you who are dissatisfied hold the right side in the dispute, there is still no single good reason for precipitate action. Intelligence, patriotism, Christianity and a firm reliance on Him who has never yet forsaken this favored land, are still competent to adjust, in the best way, all our present difficulty. In your hands, my dissatisfied fellow-countrymen, and not in mine, is the momentous issue of civil war, The government will not assail you.

"You can have no conflict without being yourselves the aggressors. You have no oath registered in heaven to destroy the government, while I shall have the most solemn one to preserve, protect and defend it.

"I am loath to close. We are not enemies, but friends. We must not be enemies; though passion may have strained, it must not break our bonds of affection.

"The mystic chords of memory, stretching from every battle-field and patriot grave to every living heart and hearthstone, all over this broad land, will yet swell the chorus of the union, when again touched, as surely they will be by the better angels of our nature."

Topics for Papers.

1 What was the situation when this was delivered?

2 What was the south's feeling toward Lincoln and his administration?

3 Lincoln's proposed policy.

a What is it in regard to slavery?

b What if the south seizes the nation's property?

c Was this a wise policy at the time? Why?

4 Does not Lincoln admit the right of the south to dismember the government? Prove your answer.

5 Is this inaugural in harmony with Seward's "Irrepressible Conflict?" Give citations to prove your answer.

XLVIII.

THE SOUTH'S APPEAL TO THE BORDER STATES

". . . The people of the confederate states have long watched with deepest sympathy the wrongs and outrages that have been inflicted upon the citizens of a commonwealth allied to the states of the south by the strongest social, political and commercial ties, and reduced to a condition of a conquered province. . . Your citizens have been arrested and imprisoned upon no charge, and contrary to all law. . .

"The government of your chief city has been usurped by armed strangers, your legislature has been dissolved by the unlawful arrest of its members; freedom of the press and of speech has been suppressed. . . and citizens ordered to be tried by military commissions for what they may dare to speak. . . The people of the south have long wished to aid you in throwing off this foreign yoke, to enable you again to enjoy the inalienable rights of freemen. . .

"In obedience to this wish, our army has come among you. . . . We know no enemies among you, and will protect all of you in every opinion.

". . . While the southern people will welcome you to your natural position among them, they will only welcome you when you come of your own free will."—*Gen. Lee* to the people of Maryland, Sept. 1862.

". . . We come, not as conquerors or despoilers, but to restore to you the liberties of which you have been deprived by a relentless foe. We come to guarantee to all the sanctity of their homes and altars; to punish with a rod of iron the despoilers of your peace and to avenge the cowardly insults to your women. . .

"Believing that the heart of Kentucky is with us in our great struggle for constitutional freedom, we have transferred from our own soil to yours . . . a powerful and well disciplined army. Your gallant Buckner leads the van. Marshall is on the right, while Breckenridge . . . is advancing with Kentucky's valiant sons to receive the honor and applause due to their heroism. . . Will you remain indifferent to our call, or will you vindicate the fair fame of your once free and envied state? We believe you will. . . .

"We have come with joyous hopes. Let us not depart in sorrow, as we shall, if we find you wedded . . . to your present lot. If you prefer federal rule show it by your frowns. . .

"Women of Kentucky! Your persecutions and heroic bearings have reached our ears. . . Buckle on the armor of your kindred, your husbands, sons, and brothers, and scoff with shame him who would prove recreant in his duty to you, his country and his God."—*Gen. Bragg* to the people of Kentucky, Sept., 1862.

Topics for Papers.

1 What do you infer was the common purpose of these addresses?

2 Enumerate the common arguments the generals used.

3 How do you account for the fact that the federal government had been so hard on Maryland?

4 What does General Lee mean by Maryland and the south being allied by common ties? Were the south and the Kentuckians so allied? Explain.

5 Since Lee and Bragg did not remain long in these states, what inferences can you draw?

XLIX.

ENGLISH OPINION ON THE CIVIL WAR

(*Blackwood's Magazine*, v. 91, pp. 129–30, Jan. 1862.)

"The questions of the recognition of the southern confederacy and the raising of the ineffectual blockade, in conjunction with France, are entitled to be immediately considered. As it is, our neutrality tells against the south. . . . If we are . . . certain of the captiousness and hostility of the north, let us at least do something to secure the friendship of the south.

"And the south, so far as can be seen, deserve recognition, independence, and sympathy. Their only crime has been a desire to take no further part in a system to which not even the letter, far less the spirit, of the law can prove that they were bound by any principle stronger than convenience, and the operation of which they declare to have been intolerably oppressive. It is natural that they should object to accept an Abraham Lincoln as their chief man, and to have their destinies influenced by such a cabinet and mob as that of the north, when, as they have shown, they can do so much better for themselves. They have chosen as president a man of judgment and conduct, who can give to their impulses unity of action, and can both excite and control their enthusiasm. . . A war between England and the north will, at least, have the good effects of shortening the sufferings and hastening the independence of a people who are proving themselves very capable of self-government, who will at once assume a creditable position among nations, and who will act as a permanent check on northern turbulence. And it is to be hoped that if war it is to be, we may put our whole strength and will into it, and conduct it so as to leave the orators and writers of the north . . . no possibility of turning its incidents to our disadvantage and to their own glorification."

(*Quarterly Review*, London, April, 1862, p. 273.)

"At all events they are now undeceived as to the real attitude of England. They must see that it is dangerous to try her patience too far. . . . But in the meantime if, as we believe will be the case, the confederate states are strong enough to maintain a separate government . . . and hold their own against all the efforts of the north, the question will seriously occur how long the recogition of their independence by foreign powers is to be delayed."

(Johnston, *Representative American Orations*, v. 3, pp. 213-42.)

". . . But I do say that your own children . . . ought to be nearer to you than any people of a strange tongue (a voice : 'Degenerate sons, applause and hisses ; another voice : 'What about the Trent ?'). If there had been any feelings of bitterness in America, let me tell you, they had been excited, rightly or wrongly, under the impression that Great Britain was going to intervene between us and our lawful struggle (a voice: 'No !' and applause). With the evidence that there is no such intention all bitter feeling will pass away (applause) . . . and we say that the utterance of Lord Russell at Blairgowrie (applause, hisses, and a voice : 'What about Lord Brougham ?'), together with the declaration of the government in stopping war-steamers here (great uproar, and applause) has gone far toward quieting every fear and removing every apprehension from our minds (uproar and shouts of applause) . . . And although I am in spirit perfectly willing to answer any question, and more than glad of the chance, yet I am by this very unnecessary opposition to-night incapacitated physically from doing it."—*Henry Ward Beecher*, at Liverpool, Eng., Oct., 1863.

THE TRENT AFFAIR

(Nicolay and Hay's Abraham Lincoln, v. 5, pp. 27, 28, 30, 39.)

" . . . The Washington government should be told that what has been done is a violation of international law and of the rights of Great Britain, and that your Majesty's government trust that the act will be disavowed, and the prisoners set free and restored to British protection; and that Lord Lyons should be instructed that, if this demand is refused, he should retire from the United States."—*Lord Palmerston* to the Queen.

"He (Prince Albert) could eat no breakfast and looked very wretched. But still he was well enough on getting up to make a draft for me to write to Lord Russell in correction of his draft to Lord Lyons, sent me yesterday, which Albert did not approve."—*Queen's Diary.*

"My wish would be that at your first interview with Mr. Seward you should not take my dispatch with you, but should prepare him for it and ask him to settle it with the president and the cabinet what course they will propose. The next time you should bring my dispatch and read it to him fully. If he asks what will be the consequence of his refusing compliance, I think you should say that you wish to leave him and the president quite free to take their own course, and that you desire to abstain from anything like menace."—*Lord Russell* to Lord Lyons.

"If I decide this case in favor of my own government I must disavow its most cherished principles, and reverse and forever abandon its essential policy . . . If I maintain those principles and adhere to that policy, I must surrender the case itself. . . The four persons in question are now held in military custody at Fort Warren. . . They will be cheerfully liberated."—*Secretary Seward* to Lord Lyons.

Topics for Papers.

1 Enumerate reasons given for recognizing independence of the south?

2 What conclusions can be drawn from Beecher's speech?

3 State the difference between the attitude of the cabinet and of Victoria and Prince Albert toward America on account of the Trent affair.

4 Which attitude was presented to the American government? Prove your answer.

5 Why did our government surrender the prisoners?

6 To what principles and policy does Secretary Seward refer and when did our government assert them?

L.

LINCOLN'S ANSWER TO GREELEY'S PRAYER

(Lincoln's Works, v. 2, pp. 227–228.)

" . . . I have not meant to leave any one in doubt. I would save the Union. I would save it the shortest way under the constitution. The sooner the national authority can be restored, the nearer the Union will be 'the Union as it was.'

If there be those who would not save the Union unless they could at the same time save slavery, I do not agree with them. If there be those who would not save the Union unless they could at the same time destroy slavery, I do not agree with them. My paramount object . . . is to save the Union, and not either to save or destroy slavery. . .

"What I do about slavery and the colored race I do because I believe it helps to save this Union; and what I forbear I forbear because I do not believe it would help save the Union. . .

"I have here stated my purpose according to my views of official duty; and I intend no modification of my oft-expressed personal wish that all men everywhere could be free."

LINCOLN'S RESPONSE TO THE CHICAGO MINISTERS

(Lincoln's Works, v. 2, p. 234–236.)

"The subject presented in the memorial is one upon which I have thought much for weeks past, and I may even say for months. . . What good would a proclamation of emancipation from me do, especially as we are now situated? . . . Would my word free the slaves, when I cannot even enforce the constitution in the rebel states? . . . Understand, I raise no objections against it on legal or constitutional grounds, for, as commander-in-chief of the army and navy in time of war I suppose I have a right to take any measure which may best subdue the enemy ; nor do I urge objections of a moral nature, in view of possible consequences of insurrection and massacre at the south. . . I have not decided against a proclamation of liberty to the slaves. . . And I can assure you that the subject is on my mind, by day and night more than any other. Whatever shall appear to be God's will, I will do. . ."

Topics for Papers.

1 What is meant by the expression "the Union as it was?" What class of men made it a motto? Why?

2 Enumerate the different views held in regard to union and slavery. Who held these views?

3 Try to justify Lincoln's paramount object.

4 What objections did Lincoln find to freeing the slaves?

5 As slavery was a legal institution, how could Lincoln say he had no legal objections to abolishing it?

LI.

BORDER STATE SENTIMENT, 1861–62

(Congressional Globe.)

MR. KELLEY *of Pennsylvania*—It is stated to be the purpose of a majority of this house to Africanize American society. Sir, that is not the object of any man on this floor.

MR. WADSWORTH *of Kentucky*—We want to know of the north if they are going to unclasp the loving arms of Kentucky and fling her into that vortex which has swallowed so many kindred states? The worst course you can pursue . . . is to attempt to confiscate the slaves or other property of the inhabitants of the rebel states.

GARRETT DAVIS *of Kentucky*—You propose to place arms in the hands of the men and boys, . . . and to manumit the whole mass, men, women and children, and leave them among us. Do you expect us to give our sanction and approval to these things? *No, no!* We would regard their authors as our worst enemies; and there is no foreign despotism that could come to our rescue that we would not joyously embrace. . . But before we had invoked this foreign despotism we would arm every man and boy . . . and we would meet you in the death grapple.

Mr. Fouke *of Illinois*—It is true . . . that a majority of the Illinois troops . . . have been enlisted south of the center line of the state. . . . The political predilections of a majority of them from that section of the state are opposed to those of the present administration, and, while they have rallied with entire unanimity in support of the government, they are now and will ever remain unalterably opposed to bestowing their energies in a war for the emancipation of the slaves.

Mr. Riddle *of Ohio*—The result of this war is freedom for all. Every day of its continuance, every dragging moment, makes this end the more inevitable. Every step on slave soil, every battle fought, no matter with what temporary result, every musket fired, every sword brandished, every soldier that suffers, and every heart that mourns, but makes this result the more absolute.

Mr. Noell *of Missouri*—But it is the weakness of cowards. . . . that now lifts up weak hands in helpless horror and raises querulous voices in feeble wails and cries for mercy to the rebels. Mercy is now treason, rape, arson, an infraction of the whole decalogue.

Mr. Lane *of Kansas*—I deny that this government cannot take the slaves of the loyal and disloyal, and that they are estopped from making any use of them that they choose for the suppression of this rebellion, and having made use of them, I say it would be a crime before God to return them to slavery.

Topics for Papers.

1 What was the nature of the change in the purpose of the war that some feared ?

2 Enumerate the variety of sentiment prevailing among border state men. Account for this variety.

3 Does not Riddle contradict Kelley ? Prove your answer.

LII.

LINCOLN'S REPLY TO THE ALBANY RESOLUTIONS

(Abraham Lincoln. *Complete works*: ed. by Nicolay and Hay, v. 2. p. 349, 363.)

". . . It is asserted in substance, that Mr. Vallandigham was, by a military commander, seized and tried 'for no other reason than words addressed to a public meeting in criticism of the course of the administration, and in condemnation of the military orders of the general.' Now, if there be no mistake about this . . . if there was no other reason for the arrest, then I concede that the arrest was wrong . . . Mr. Vallandigham avows his hostility to the war on the part of the Union ; and his arrest was made because he was laboring, with some effect, to prevent the raising of troops, to encourage desertion from the army, and to leave the rebellion without an adequate military force to suppress it. He was not arrested because he was damaging the political prospects of the administration or the personal interests of the commanding general, but because he was damaging the army, upon the existence and vigor of which the life of the nation depends. . . .

"I understand the meeting whose resolutions I am considering to be in favor of suppressing the rebellion by military force—by armies. Long experience has shown that armies cannot be maintained unless desertions shall be punished by the severe penalty of death. The case requires, and the law and the constitution sanction, this punishment. Must I shoot a simple-minded soldier boy who deserts, while I must not touch a hair of a wily agitator who induces him to desert? This is none the less injurious when effected by getting a father, or brother, or friend into a public meeting, and there working upon his feelings till he is persuaded to write the soldier boy that he is fighting in a bad cause, for a wicked administration of a contemptible government, too weak to arrest and punish him if he shall desert. I think that, in such a case, to silence the agitator and save the boy is not only constitutional, but withal a great mercy. . . ."

LINCOLN'S REPLY TO THE OHIO COMMITTEE

". . . Your own attitude, therefore, encourages desertion, resistance to the draft, and the like. . . .

"After a short personal intercourse with you, gentlemen of the committee, I cannot say I think you desire this effect to follow your attitude; but I assure you that both friends and enemies of the Union look upon it in this light. It is a substantial hope . . . to the enemy. If it is a false hope and one which you would willingly dispel, I will make the way exceedingly easy.

"I send you duplicates of this letter in order that you, or a majority of you, may, if you choose, indorse your names upon one of them and return it thus indorsed to me with the understanding that those signing are thereby committed to the following propositions and to nothing else :

"1 That there is now a rebellion in the United States, the object and tendency of which is to destroy the national Union ; and that, in your opinion, an army and navy are constitutional means for suppressing that rebellion ;

"2 That no one of you will do anything which, in his own judgment, will tend to hinder the increase, or favor the decrease, or lessen the efficiency of the army or navy, while engaged in the effort to suppress that rebellion ; and

"3 That each of you will, in his sphere, do all

he can to have the officers, soldiers, and seamen of the army and navy, while engaged in the effort to suppress the rebellion, paid, fed, clad, and otherwise well provided for and supported.

"And with the further understanding that upon receiving the letter and names thus indorsed, I will cause them to be published, which publication shall be, within itself, a revocation of the order in relation to Mr. Vallandigham."

Topics for Papers.

1 What was the alleged, and what was the real reason for Vallandigham's arrest?

2 What constitutional questions did his arrest raise?

3 Show the contradiction between the acts and the professions of the Albany meeting.

4 Show how the attitude of the Ohio committee encouraged desertions and opposition to the draft.

5 Why did the Ohio committee not sign the propositions?

LIII.

EXTRACTS BEARING ON THE RESTORATION OF THE UNION

"In my correspondence with Mr. Lincoln, that functionary has always spoken of the United

States and the confederacy as 'Our afflicted country;' but, in my replies, I have never failed to refer to them as separate and distinct governments; and, sooner than we should ever be united again, I would be willing to yield up everything I have on earth, and, if it were possible, would sacrifice my life a thousand times before I would succumb."—*Jefferson Davis*, Feb., 1865.

"That we approve the determination of the government of the United States not to compromise with rebels, nor to offer them any terms of peace except such as may be based upon an unconditional surrender of their hostility and a return to their just allegiance to the constitution and the laws of the United States.

"That, as slavery was the cause and now constitutes the strength of this rebellion, and as it must be always and everywhere hostile to the principles of republican government, justice and the national safety demand its utter and complete extirpation from the soil of the republic."—*Republican platform*, 1864.

"That in the future, as in the past, we will adhere with unswerving fidelity to the union under the constitution, as the only solid foundation of our strength, security and happiness as a people, and as a framework of government equally conducive to the welfare and prosperity of all the states, both northern and southern.

"*Resolved*, That the aim and object of the democratic party is to preserve the federal union and the rights of the states unimpaired ; and they hereby declare that they consider the administrative usurpation of extraordinary and dangerous powers not granted by the constitution, the subversion of the civil by military law in states not in insurrection, the arbitrary military arrest, imprisonment, trial, and sentence, of American citizens in states where civil law exists in full force, the suppression of freedom of speech and of the press, the denial of the right of asylum, the open and avowed disregard of state rights, the employment of unusual test oaths, and the interference with and denial of the right of the people to bear arms, as calculated to prevent a restoration of the Union and the perpetuation of a government deriving its just powers from the consent of the governed."—*Democratic platform*, 1864.

"The re-establishment of the Union, in all its integrity, is and must continue to be the indispensable condition in any settlement. So soon as it is clear, or even probable, that our present adversaries are ready for peace upon the basis of the Union, we should exhaust all the resources of statesmanship practiced by civilized nations and taught by the traditions of the American people, consistent with the honor and interests of the country, to secure such peace, re-establish the Union, and guarantee for the future the constitutional rights of every state. The Union is

the one condition of peace. We ask no more. . . I could not look in the face my gallant comrades of the army and navy who have survived so many bloody battles, and tell them that their labors and the sacrifice of so many of our slain and wounded brethren had been in vain—that we had abandoned that Union for which we have so often periled our lives. A vast majority of our people, whether in the army and navy, or at home, would, as *I* would, hail with unbounded joy the permanent restoration of peace on the basis of the Union under the constitution, without the effusion of another drop of blood ; but *no peace can be permanent without union. . .*"
—*Gen. McClellan*, Letter of acceptance.

Topics for Paper.

1 State the difference between the above extracts with reference to the way in which the union was to be restored.

2 Keeping in mind the position of Davis, which of the other methods of restoration were possible? Why?

3 Enumerate the causes, given in the democratic platform, which tend to prevent a restoration of the union.

4 State the difference between the parties in their interpretation of the constitution.

LIV.

COLLAPSE OF THE CONFEDERACY

(Extracts from the Diary of a Rebel War Clerk.)

"To-day, I saw two conscripts from western Virginia conducted to the cars going to Lee's army *in chains.* It made a chill shoot through my breast.

"Lee writes that the Bureau of Conscription fails to replenish the army. The rich men and slave-owners get out and keep out of the service. Nearly every landed proprietor has given bonds to furnish meal to obtain exemption. Over 100,000 landed proprietors, and most of the slave-owners, are now out of the ranks, and soon, I fear, we shall have an army that will not fight, having nothing to fight for. The higher class is staying at home making money, the lower is thrust into the trenches. Lee complains that the rich young men are elected magistrates to avoid service in the field. Guards everywhere in the city are arresting pedestrians, and forcing them into the army. The militia are all out except those hidden in the back rooms of their shops. . . Colonel Gardner reports that of the citizens taken from the streets to the front last week, a majority have deserted—that despotic order is the theme of universal execration. Brigadier-General Preston, of the Bureau of Conscription, says there are now 100,000 deserters. . . The books of the conscript office show a frightful list of deserters—60,000 Virginians. . . The poor men in the army can get nothing for their families, and there is a prospect of their starving.

"General Early's cavalry, being mostly men of property, were two-thirds of them on furlough or detail, when the enemy advanced on Charlottesville, and the infantry, being poor, with no means either to bribe the authorities, to fee members of congress, or to aid their suffering families, declined to fight in defense of the property of the rich and *absent* neighbors!

. . . With reference to the employment of negroes as soldiers, I think the measure not only expedient but necessary . . I do not think our white population can supply the necessities of a long war without taxing its capacity and imposing great suffering upon our people . . . I think those who are employed should be freed. It would neither be just nor wise to require them to serve as slaves."—*General R. E. Lee*, Feb. 18, 1865.

"I saw a captain, a commissary, give his dog a piece of beef for which I would have paid a dollar. Many little children of soldiers were standing by with empty baskets. A poor woman yesterday applied to a merchant in Carey Street to purchase a barrel of flour. The price he demanded was $70. 'My God! ' exclaimed she, 'how can I pay such prices? I have seven children. What shall I do?' 'I don't know, madam,' said he, coolly, 'unless you eat your children!'"

Major Ferguson having got permission of the Quartermaster-General to sell me a suit of cloth—there being a piece too dark for the army, I got . . . enough for coat, pants and vest at $12 per yard—the price in the stores is $125; and I have the promise of the government tailor to make it up for some $30 or $40, the ordinary price being $350 . . . Tom has bought a new black coat made before the war, for $175 . . . And my daughter Anne has made three fine bonnets, . . . from the débris of old ones; the price of these would be $700. So I fear not but we shall be fed and clad by the providence of God.

Dec. 30, 1864 . . . I saw selling at auction, to-day, second-hand shirts at $40 each and blankets at $75. A bedstead, such as I have bought for $10 brought $700.

January 2d, 1865.—Offered the owner of our servant $400 per annum. He wants $150 and clothing. Clothing would cost perhaps $1,000. It remains in abeyance.

January 6th.—Corn-meal has risen from $50 up to $75 per bushel. Flour to $500 per barrel.

January 9th.—Flour is $700 per barrel to-day;

meal $80 per bushel; coal and wood $100 per load. Does the government (alone to blame) mean to allow the rich speculators, the quartermasters, etc., to starve honest men into the Union?

January 14th.—Flour is $1,000 per barrel to-day.

January 18th.—Flour is $1,256 per barrel to-day.

January 27th.—My wood-house was broken into last night and two (of the nine) sticks of wood taken. Wood is selling at $5 a stick this cold morning; mercury at zero.

DESPOTISM OF THE CONFEDERATE GOVERNMENT.

(Johnson and Browne's *Life of A. H. Stephenson.*)

"I am satisfied that I can do no good here. . . I have strong inclinations to resign. . . . I shall do nothing hastily or rashly, but I can never approve doctrines and principles which are likely to become fixed in this country. . . . If this bill passes (bill to suspend habeas corpus). . . . I do trust that Governor Brown will issue his proclamation advising the justices of the inferior courts to disregard it until the matter may be adjudicated by our own supreme court. If that court shall decide the act to be constitutional, I shall feel very little further interest in the result of the conflict. It will simply be a conflict between dynasties—a struggle between two powers,—not for rights or constitutional liberty, but for despotism."—*Vice-Pres. Stephenson,* Dec. 1864.

Topics for Papers.

1 What was the fundamental cause of frequent and severe conscriptions in the south ?

2 What reasons exempted one from conscription !

3 Enumerate motives of different classes for desertion or exemption.

4 What proofs do you find that this was "a rich man's war and a poor man's fight ?"

5 What reasons can you discover for the rapid rise in prices in the south ?

6 What inferences can be drawn from the Vice-President Stephenson's words ?

LV.

THE KUKLUX KLAN.

(U. S.—House. 42d. cong. 2d. sess. *Report of Committee,* No. 22, pt. 1, p. 23, 48.)

Presentment of U. S. grand jury, Columbia, S: C.

. . . That there has existed since 1868 . . . an organization known as the 'Kuklux

Klan' or 'Invisible empire of the south,' which embraces in its membership a large proportion of the white population of every profession and class. . .

"I (name) before the immaculate Judge of Heaven and Earth, and upon the holy evangelists of Almighty God, do, of my own free will and accord, subscribe to the following sacredly binding obligation.

"1 We are on the side of justice, humanity, and constitutional liberty, as bequeathed to us in its purity by our forefathers.

"2 We oppose and reject the principles of the radical party.

"3 We pledge mutual aid to each other in sickness, distress, and pecuniary embarrassment.

"4 . . . Any member divulging, or causing to be divulged, any of the foregoing obligations, shall meet the fearful penalty and traitor's doom, which is Death! Death! Death!

" . . . That the Klan . . . inflicted summary vengeance on the colored citizens of these countries, by breaking into their houses at the dead of night, dragging them from their beds, torturing them in the most inhuman manner, and in many instances murdering them; and this, mainly, on account of their political affiliations."

Testimony of James M. Justice, native of North Carolina.

"He (the chief of the Klan) then commenced telling how mean I had been in supporting the republican party, and advocating principles that gave negroes the right to vote and hold office, and asked me if I did not know that the constitution, as they had it before negroes were free, was better . . . 'and we are going to kill all men like you who advocate and support any such government or constitution. . . I have come here to-night with positive orders to take your life ; it has been decreed in camp.'"

THE CARPET-BAGGERS

Testimony of Gen. James H. Clanton, Alabama.

"If a man should come there and invest $100,000, and in the next year should seek the highest office by appealing to the basest prejudices of an ignorant race, we would call him a political carpet-bagger. But if he followed his legitimate business . . . behaved himself . . . we should call him a gentleman. Gen. Warner bought land. . . Before his seat in Ohio had got cold he was running the negro machine among us to put himself in office. . . But he came just after, if not before, his senatorial term in Ohio expired, and by ring, in with the negroes, attained that position."

Testimony of Gen. Wright, Georgia.

"They (negroes) were taken possession of by a class of men . . . in some way connected with the Freedmen's bureau; they swarmed all over the country. They made the negroes believe that unless they banded themselves together . . . the white people would put them back into slavery. . . Up to the latter part of 1868 that by voting they were going to get a division of the land and stock of the country. These carpet-baggers would go down there and actually sell stakes to them . . . but these rascals would . . . sell painted stakes to these negroes, and tell them that all they had to do was to put down the stakes on their owners' farms, and forty acres of land would be theirs after the election."

Topics for Papers.

1 What do you infer as to

a Nature of the Kuklux organization?

b Its purposes?

c Its work?

2 Enumerate the causes, discovered above, of such an organization.

3 Carpet-baggers.

a Who were they?

b Enumerate their faults.

c Was it possible for them to do any good?

Books for Teaching History.

1. *A Thousand Questions in American History.* Cloth, 16mo, pp. 247. Price $1.00.

This work shows rare breadth of view and discrimination, dealing not merely with events but with causes, and with the side-issues that have so much to do with determining the destiny of a nation.

2. *Helps in Fixing the Facts of American History.* By HENRY C. NORTHAM. Cloth, 16mo, pp. 298. Price $1.00.

Here all facts are presented in groups. The key-word to the Revolution, for instance, is LIBERTY, as shown in the accompanying table of *Key-Words;* and in like manner the events of the late civil war are kept chronologically distinct by the key-words SLAVES FREED. Chart No. 1 indicates by stars the years in each decade from 1492 to 1789, in which the most remarkable events occurred, while the colored chart No. 2 arranges the events in 12 groups.

L—exington.
I—ndependence.
B—urgoyne's Surrender.
E—vacuation.
R—etribution.
T—reason.
Y—orktown

3. *Outline and Topic Book in U. S. History.* Paper, 8vo, pp. 212. 50 cts.

The true and normal method of teaching any study is by the use of topics. The great demand in school work to-day is a system that will stimulate pupils to investigate subjects, and train them to report the results of their investigation in a clear, logical, and forcible manner, using their own language rather than repeating the words of the text-book. To this end, this book has been prepared. The important events are emphasized, and references are made on each topic to fifteen School Histories, giving the page or pages in each on which the subject is treated. Blank leaves have been inserted for the convenience of those using the book who may wish to add such points as their own experience may suggest. This book will be found of great value, not only in daily recitations, but in weekly and monthly reviews.

4. *Topics and References in American History*, with numerous Search Questions. By GEO. A. WILLIAMS. Leatherette, 16mo, pp. 50. 50 cts.

The references are largely to the lighter and more interesting illustrations of history, of a kind to arouse the thought of pupils by giving vivid conceptions of the events narrated. By dividing these references among the members of a class, the history recitation may be made the most delightful of the day.

5 *Brief Views of United States History.* By ANNA M. JULIAND. *New edition, broaght down to 1882.* Leatherette, 16mo, pp. 69, 35 cts.

It contains the leading facts chronologically arranged under the various administrations, leaving the story to be filled out from reference-books.

6. *Outlines and Questions in United States History.* By C. B. VAN WIE. Paper, 16mo, pp. 40, and folding map. 15 cts.

7. *Dime Question Books, No. 5, General History*, and *No. 6, United States History and Civil Government.* By ALBERT P. SOUTHWICK. Paper, 16mo, pp. 37, 32. 10 cts. each.

C. W. BARDEEN, Publisher, Syracuse, N. Y.

Cards and Charts for Teaching History.

1. *Historical Cards*, with Topics, Questions, and References on the most important events in *General History*, 200 cards, 3¼ x 5¼ inches, in box, $1.00.

These cards are designed for use in the High and College Preparatory Schools.

On each card is a topic, with subdivisions and questions. On the back of each card reference is made to all the leading histories used in the schools of the country. *Thousands of references are cited.* Space has been left on each card for additional questions and references.

The cards may be used in daily recitations and reviews. In addition to the many Histories cited, a large number of books are referred to under the head of "Interesting Reading." Different colors are used for the several Historical Epochs.

2, *Historical Cards*, with Topics, Questions, and References on all the important events in *United States History*. 200 cards, 3¼ x 5¼ inches, in box $1.00. Or,

Part I. Prehistoric Period, Period of Discoveries and Explorations, Period of Settlements, Period of the Revolutionary War. 92 cards, in box, 50 cts.

Part II. Constitutional Period, which includes the Periods of the Development of the States, the Civil War, Reconstruction, and more recent events, General Review, Civil Government. 108 cards, in box, 50 cts.

On each card there is a topic, with subdivisions and questions. On the back of the cards reference is made to fifteen School Histories, giving the page or pages in each on which the subject is in any way treated. Nearly 5,000 references are cited. The cards may be used with any United States History. The topics and questions are so arranged that the pupils, in reciting, must necessarily express themselves in their own language, rather than that of the book. Much time is saved the teacher in having the topics prepared. Different colors are used for the several Historical Epochs.

3. *A Chart of United States History*, By NOAH T. CLARKE, Ph.D. One page, 9x12. Each 5 cts.; per dozen 50 cts.

This chart gives a birdseye view of the entire history of our country. No more practically helpful review has ever been published.

4. *Conspectus of United States History* to the time of Garfield. Cloth, 81x91 inches, on rollers. $2.00.

5. *Conspectus of the History of Political Parties and the Federal Government* to 1880. By WALTER R. HOUGHTON. Cloth, 4to, pp. 85, with colored charts, $5.00. Or chart alone, mounted on rollers, $1.00.

6. *Syllabusses of American History.* By WELLAND HENDRICK. Paper, 8vo, pp. 4. Each 5 cts. Per dozen 50 cts.

Published four times a year, for the Regents' Examinations.

C. W. BARDEEN, Publisher, Syracuse, N. Y.

The School Bulletin

AND NEW YORK STATE EDUCATIONAL JOURNAL,

Established 1874. 24 *pages,* 9 x 14. $1.00 *a year.*

The *School Bulletin* is one of the five oldest educational journals in America, and the only one of them that has been under the same ownership and management from the beginning. It was the only American School journal which received the gold medal at the Paris Exposition of 1889, and it received the highest award offered at the Chicago Exposition of 1893, the diploma pronouncing it "of the greatest interest and historical value to educators of all grades". It is not filled with "methods" and spoon-food for young teachers who want their ideas ready-made, but appeals to superintendents, principals, and all teachers who regard their work as a vocation, and who want to look upon it broadly and comprehensively.

In the feature of educational news it has never had a rival. Its chronicles of what has happened in New York schools since its establishment are unmatched in educational literature, and it has taken note of whatever has happened in other States that involved general principles.

Its Current Topics give a chronicle of what occured during the preceding month with forcible terseness, and in a perspective that bring the important events clearly to the front, adding maps wherever necessary. For the instruction of classes in this branch, now commonly recognized as essential, and for preparation of teachers' examinations, the Current Topics as here presented have been declared to be the best anywhere to be found. In New York they are of especial value in preparation for the Uniform Examinations, as the *Bulletin* is issued *every* month of the year (not for ten months only), at such a date that it will reach New York subscribers just before the Uniform Examination of the month, and thus present the news fresh and up to date.

It publishes each month all the Uniform Examination questions and answers of the preceding month, with all the illustrations in drawing and other subjects. It publishes all the questions given at the examinations for State Certificates; all the circulars and legal decisions issued by the Department of Public Instruction; and has indeed two Official Departments edited and conducted by members of the Department of Public Instruction and of the Regents, respectively.

It is therefore primarily an educational journal for New York teachers, and is meant to be a journal no New York teacher can afford to be without. But teachers in other States will find it of great service, both for the intrinsic value of its contents, and for the vivid picture it gives of educational progress in the Empire State.

C. W. BARDEEN, Publisher, Syracuse, N. Y.

p , vo, pp. 25

McCully's *Perforated Erasers*, per doz............................. 1 00

McKay (John S.) *100 Experiments in Natural Science.* Paper, 16mo, pp. 50 15

***Maps for the Wall.** Send for Special Circulars.

Maps **Relief Maps.* Switzerland, 11x17½, $3.50; 23x34, $10.00. Palestine.. 10 00

——*Dissected Maps.* United States sawn into States.......................... 75

——*The same*, New York State sawn into Counties.......................... 75

——**Onondaga County.* Cloth, 4x4½ feet.......... ....10 00

——*New York State.* Cloth, 61x76 inches........... .... 5 00

Marble (A. P.) *Powers of School Officers.* Paper. 16mo, pp. 27.......... 15

Marenholz-Buelow (Baroness) *School Work-shops.* Paper, 16mo, pp. 27. 15

——*Child and Child Nature.* Frœbel's Ed'l Theories. Cloth, 12mo, pp. 207.. 1 50

Maudsley (H.) *Sex in Mind and Education.* Paper, 16mo, pp. 42..... 15

Maxwell (W. H.) *Examinations as Tests for Promotion.* Paper, 8vo, pp. 11 15

——*The Text-Books of Comenius*, with cuts from the *Orbis Pictus.* 8vo, pp. 24 25

Meiklejohn (J. M. D.) *The New Education.* 16mo, pp. 35 15

——*An old Educational Reformer.* Dr. Andrew Bell. Cloth, 16mo, pp. 182... 1 00

Michael (O. S.) *Algebra for Beginners.* Cloth, 16mo, pp. 120............... 75

Mill (John Stuart.) *Inaugural Address at St. Andrews.* Paper, 8vo, pp. 31... 25

Miller (Warner.) *Education as a Dep't of Government.* Paper, 8vo, pp. 12. 15

Mills (C. D. B.) *The Tree of Mythology.* Cloth, 8vo, Pp. 281... .... 3 00

Milne (James M.) *Teachers' Institutes, Past and Present.* Paper, 8vo, pp. 22.. 25

Milton (John) *A Small Tractate of Education.* Paper, 16mo, pp. 26....... 15

——*Sketch of*, by R. H. Quick. Paper, 16mo, pp 55 15

Minutes *of the International Congress of Education*, 1889. Cloth, 4 vols...... 5 00

Missouri, *Civil Government of*, Northam. Cloth, 16mo, pp 151............. 75

Monroe (Will S.) *Labors of Henry Barnard.* Leath , 16mo, pp. 35........ 50

New York *Question Book*, with all the Questions of the Uniform, State, Cornell, Scholarship, and Normal Entrance Examinations, to March 31, 1890, *with Answers.* 8vo, pp. 461. Cloth $2 00; paper........... .... 1 00

——*The same*, Supplement No. 1, to June, 1891. Manilla, 8vo, pp. 63.. 25

——*The same*, Supplement No. 2, to June, 1892. Manilla, 8vo, pp. 139.... ... 25

——*The same*, Questions in Drawing to Date. Paper, 16mo, pp. 92. 25

——*The same*, Questions in Civil Gov't and School Law. Paper, 16mo. 25

——*The same*, Questions in Methods and School Economy. Manilla, 16mo.. 50

——*The same*, Questions in Geography. 16mo.................................. 50

——*State Examination Questions* to date. Cloth, 16mo, pp. 402..... .... 1 00

——*The Questions in Book-Keeping, with Answers.* Paper, 16mo, pp. 31..... 10

——*History of the Empire State*, Hendrick. Cloth, 12mo, pp. 203 75

——*Civil Government of the State of*, Northam. Cloth, 16mo, pp. 185........ 75

——*Code of Public Instruction.* Latest Edition.................................. 2 50

——*Natural History*, and *Cabinet Reports.* Write for information.

Northam (Henry C.) *Civil Government.* Cloth, 16mo, pp. 231............ 75

——*The same for Missouri.* Cloth, 16mo, pp. 151.............................. 75

——*Fixing the Facts of American History.* Cloth, 16mo, pp. 300............. 75

——*Conversational Lessons Leading to Geography.* Paper, 16mo, pp. 39...... 25

Northend (Chas.) *Memory Selections.* Three series. Each.. 25

——*The Parent and Teacher.* Cloth, 16mo, pp. 350. .... 1 00

Northrop (B. G.) *High Schools.* Paper, 8vo, pp. 26............................ 25

Northrup (A. J.) *Camps and Tramps in the Adirondacks.* 16mo, pp. 302. 1 25

Number Lessons. On card-board, 7x11, after the Grube Method.......... 10

Oswald (John). *Dictionary of English Etymology.* Cloth, 16mo, pp. 806... 2 00

Page (David P.) *The Theory and Practice of Teaching.* Cloth, 16mo, pp. 448. 1 00

Pardon (Emma L.) *Oral Instruction in Geography.* Paper, 16mo, pp. 29.... 15

Parsons (James Russell, Jr.,) *Prussian Schools.* Cloth, 8vo, pp. 91......... 1 00

——*French Schools through American Eyes.* Cloth, 8vo, pp. 130.......... 1 00

Payne (Joseph.) *Lectures on the Art of Education.* Cloth, 16mo, pp. 281.. 1 00

Payne (W. H.) *A Short History of Education.* Cloth, 16mo, pp. 105.... 50

Pedagogical Primers. Manilla, 16mo, pp. 40, each 25

1. School Management, pp. 45. 2. Letter-Writing, pp. 37.

Perez (B.) *The First Three Years of Childhood.* Cloth, 16mo, pp. 295....... 1 50

——*Tiedemann's Record of Infant Life.* Manilla, pp. 46........... 15

Periodicals. *The School Bulletin.* Monthly, 16 pp., 10x14. Per year....... 1 00

—— Bound Vols. I-XX. Cloth, 200 pp., each..................................... 2 00

——*The Hamilton Declamation Quarterly* Per year 1 00

——*The School Room.* Bound volumes I-V. Each.............................. 1 50

——*The New Education.* Vol. VI.. 2 00

Pestalozzi (J. H.) *His Aim and Work*, by De Guimps. 12mo, pp. 296...... 1 50

——*Sketch of*, by R. H. Quick. Paper, 16mo, pp. 40....... 15

——*How Gertrude Teaches her Children.* Cloth, 12mo, pp. 320.......... 1 5
——*Pestalozzian Arithmetics.* 16mo, 1st Year, pp. 217. 2d Year, pp. 236. Each 5
——*Lessons on Number and Form*, by C. Reiner. Cloth, 16mo, pp. 439...... 3 0
Pick (Dr. E.) *Dr. Pick's French Method.* Leatherette, 16mo, pp. 118...... 1 0
——*Memory, and the Rational Means of Improving it.* Cloth, 16mo, pp. 193... 1 0
Pitcher (James.) *Outlines of Surveying and Navigation.* Cloth, 16mo, pp. 121 5
Plumb (Chas. G.) *Map Drawing of New York.* Manilla, 8vo, pp. 16........ 2
Pooler (Chas. T.) *Chart of Civil Government.* Sheets 12x18, per hundred.. 5 0(
——*Hints on Teaching Orthoepy.* Paper, 16mo, pp. 15.................. 1
Preece (Mrs. Louise,) *Physical Culture. Illustrated.* Cloth, 4to. pp. 292. 2 0
Prentice (Mrs. J. B.) *Review Problems in Arithmetic.* Paper, 16mo, pp. 93. 2
——*Key to the above.* Paper, 16mo, pp. 20 2
——*Review Questions in Geography.* Paper, 16mo, pp. 48..................... 1
Primer *of School Management* and *of Letter-Writing.* Manilla, pp. 45, 37, ea. 2
Quick (R. H.) *Essays on Educational Reformers.* Cloth, 12mo, pp., 331 .... 1 5
Redway (J. W.) *School Geography of Pennsylvania.* Leather'te, 16mo, pp. 98 3
***Regents' Examination Paper.** Per 1000 half-sheets in box............ 3 0
Regents' Examination Pens. ¼ Gross, 25c. Per Gross, post-paid...... 1 00
Regents' Fourth Year Latin. *Cæsar's Conspiracy.* Paper, 16mo, pp. 20 1
Regents' Selections *in American, German, and French Literature.* Leatherette, pp. 56. 25 cents. Each separate, paper.............................. 1(
Regents' Examination Record. For 432 scholars, $3.00; 864 scholars.. 6 0
Regents' Examination Syllabus, in U. S. History. Paper, per dozen,.. 5
Regents' Questions. *To June, 1882. (No later are printed). Eleven Editions.*

1. *Complete with Key.* Cloth, 16mo, pp. 476.................................. 2 0
2. *Complete.* The same as the above, but without the answers. Pp. 333. 1 0
3. *Arithmetic.* The 1,293 questions in Arithmetic. Pp. 93.......... 2
4. *Key to Arithmetic,* Answers to the above. Manilla, 16mo, pp. 20.... 2
6. *Geography,* The 1,987 questions in Geography. Pp. 70........ 2
7. *Key to Geography.* Answers to the above. Manilla, 16mo, pp. 36.... 2
8. *Grammar.* The 2,976 questions in Grammar. Manilla, 16mo, pp. 109 2
9. *Grammar and Key.* Cloth, 16mo, pp. 198........................... 1 0
10. *Key to Grammar.* Manilla, 16mo, pp. 88................................ 2
11. *Spelling.* The 4,800 words given in Spelling. Manilla, 16mo, pp. 61. 2

Rein (W.) *Outlines of Pedagogics.* Cloth, 12mo, pp. 208. .... 1 2
Richardson (B. W.) *Learning and Health.* Paper, 16mo, pp. 39.......... 1
Robinson (A. H.) *Numeral School Register.* Manilla, folio, pp. 16........... 2
Rousseau (J. J.) *Sketch of* by R. H. Quick. Paper, 16mo, pp. 30.......... 1
Rooper (T. G.) *"A Pot of Green Feathers."* Leatherette, 16mo, pp. 591.. 5
——*Object Teaching or Words and Things.* Leatherette, 16mo, pp. 56 50
Ryan (G. W.) *School Record.* 56 blanks on each of 14 sheets............ 5
Sabin (Henry) *"Organization" vs. Individuality.* Paper, 8vo, pp. 9........ 2
Sanford (H. R.) *The Word Method in Number.* Per box of 45 cards. 5(
——*The Limited Speller.* Leatherette, 16mo, pp. 104........................ 3
Schepmoes (A. E.) *Rise of the New York School System.* Leath., 16mo, pp. 32 3
School Room Classics. 11 vols. Paper, 16mo, pp. about 40, each........ 1

I. Huntington's *Unconscious Tuition.*
II. Fitch's *Art of Questioning.*
III. Kennedy's *Philosophy of School Discipline.*
IV. Fitch's *Art of Securing Attention.*
V. Richardson's *Learning and Health.*
VI. Meiklejohn's *New Education.*
VII. Milton's *Tractate of Education.*
VIII. Von Buelow's *School Workshop.*
IX. Maudsley's *Sex in Mind and in Education.*
X. *Education as Viewed by Thinkers.*
XI. Harris's *How to Teach Natural Science in the Public Schools.*
XII. Dickinson's *Oral Teaching.*
XIII. Tiedemann's *Record of Infant Life*
XIV. Butler's *Place of Comenius in Education.*
XV. Harris's *Theory of Education.*

Schreber (D. G. R.) *Home Exercise for Health and Cure.* Cloth, 16mo, pp. 91 50
Shaw's *Scholar's Register,* Paper, 5x7, pp. 16. Per dozen................. 50
Sheely (Aaron) *Anecdotes and Humors of School Life.* Cloth, 12mo, pp. 350 1 50
Sherrill (J. E.) *The Normal Question Book.* Cloth. 12mo, pp. 405........ 1 50
Shirreff (Emily). *The Kindergarten System.* Cloth, 12mo, pp. 200.......... 1 00
Skinner (Chas. R.) *The Arbor Day Manual.* Cloth, 8vo, pp. 475 .... 2 50
——*The New York Question Book.* Cloth, 8vo, pp. 461. *See New York*......... 2 00
Smith (C. F.) *Honorary Degrees in American Colleges.* Paper, 8vo, pp. 9... 15
Smith (Edward.) *History of the Schools of Syracuse* Cloth, 8vo, pp. 347...... 3 00
Smith (Geo. M.) *Vocabulary to Cæsar's Gallic War.* Cloth, 16mo, pp. 67.. 50
Smith (Wm) *Geometry Test Papers.* Package of 100, 8½x10............. 1 00
Song Budget, *The.* 183th *Thousand.* Paper, small 4to pp. 76, ... 15
Song Century, *The.* Paper, small 4to, pp. 87............................ 15
Song Gymnast, *The.* Cloth, 16mo, pp. 160.................................. 50

Song Patriot, *The.* Paper, small 4to, pp. 80 1
Song Budget Music Series, including all the above. Cloth, pp. 243.... 5
Songs from Arbor Day Manual. Manilla, 8vo, pp. 60.......................... 2
Songs of the Lyceum League. Leatherette, 4to, pp. 48.......................... 2
Sornberger (S. J.) *Normal Language Lessons,* Boards, 16mo, pp. 75..... 5
Southwick (A. P.) *Twenty Dime Question Books,* with full answers, notes, queries, etc. Paper. 16mo, pp. about 40. Each.......................... 1

Elementary Series.

3. Physiology.
4. Theory and Practice.
6. U. S. History and Civil Gov't.
10. Algebra.
13. American Literature.
14. Grammar.
15. Orthography and Etymology
18. Arithmetic.
19. Physical and Political Geog.
20. Reading and Punctuation.

The 10 in one book, cloth, $1.00.

Advanced Series.

1. Physics.
2. General Literature.
5. General History.
7. Astronomy.
8. Mythology.
9. Rhetoric.
11. Botany.
12. Zoology.
16. Chemistry.
17. Geology.

The 10 in one book, cloth, $1.00.

——*Extra Numbers,* edited by C. W. Bardeen, 21. Temperance Physiology; 22. Book-Keeping; 23. Letter-Writing. Each.......................... 1
——*Quizzism.* Quirks and Quibbles from Queer Quarters. 16mo, pp. 25.... 2
——*A Quiz Book of Theory and Practice.* Cloth, 12mo, pp. 220.......... 1 0
Spencer (Herbert). *Education.* 16mo, pp. 300. Manilla, 50 cts.; Cloth..... 1
Standard Teachers' Library. Includes Laurie's *Comenius,* Carlisle's *Memoirs,* Page's *Theory and Practice,* DeGuimp's *Pestalozzi,* Spencer's *Education,* DeGraff's *Guide,* Tate's *Philosophy,* etc. Each, paper. 5
Steven, (Wm.) *History of the Edinburgh High School.* Cloth, 16mo, pp. 590 2 0
Stilwell (Lamont) *Practical Question Book.* Cloth, 12mo, pp. 400........ 1 5
Stowell (T. B.) *Syllabus of Lectures on Physiology.* Boards, 8vo, pp. 133.. 1 0
Straight (H. H.) *Aspects of Industrial Education.* Paper, 8vo, pp. 12..... 1
Swett (John) *Manual of Elocution.* Cloth, 12mo, pp. 300, *net*............. 1 5

Tate (Thos.) *The Philosophy of Education.* Cloth. 16mo, pp. 330....... 1 5
Taylor (H. F.) *Union School Record Cards* 5x8 inches. Per hundred.......2 0
Teacher's Mentor, *The.* Cloth. 16mo, pp. 274.......................... 1 0
Thomas (Flavel S.) *University Degrees.* Paper, 16mo, pp. 40...... 1
Thousand Questions *in U. S. History.* Cloth, 16mo, pp. 200.............. 1 0
Thoughts *from Earnest Women.* Paper, 16mo, pp. 36.......... 1
Tiedemann (D.) *Record of Infant Life.* Paper, 16mo, pp. 46............ 1
Tillinghast (Wm.) *The Diadem of School Songs.* Boards, 4to, pp. 160. ... 5

Underwood (L. M.) *Systematic Plant Record.* Manilla, 7x8¼ pp. 52...... 8
Uniform Examination Paper, for Commissioners. 500 sheets.......... 2 5C
Uniform Examination Questions, *New York,* to March 1889. Arithmetic, Geography, Grammar, U. S. History, Civil Government Physiology, and Keys to each. Each.......................... 1
☞ *See also* NEW YORK.

Van Wie (C. B.) *Outlines in U. S. History.* Paper, 16mo, pp. 40 and map 1
——*Development Helps.* Leatherette. 16mo, pp. 100.......................... 5
——*Methods in Common Branches.* Cloth, 16mo, pp. 197.......... . . 75

Weaver (E. W.) *Pictures in Language Work* Paper, 8vo, pp. 27............. 20
Welch (Emma A.) *Intermediate Arithmetic Problems.* Cloth, 16mo, pp. 172 75
——*Key* to the above, Cloth. 16mo. pp. 30.......................... 50
Wells (C. R.) *Natural Movement Series of Writing Books.* Nos. 1, 2, per dozen 84 cts. Nos. 3-5 96
——*Manual of the Movement Method in Writing.* Paper, 4to, pp. 44. *Ill.*....... 25
——*A Lesson on Arm Movement in Writing.* Paper, 8vo, pp. 32................ 25
Wheatley (Wm. A.) *German Declensions Simplified.* Paper, 16mo, pp. 53... 25
Wilkin (Eva) *Map Drawing Book of the Continents.* Boards, 4to, pp. 48, 75
——*Map Drawing Book of the United States.* Boards, pp. 37.............. 75
——*Descriptive Geography taught by means of Map Drawing.* Teachers' Edition. Boards, 4to, pp. 129. with 49 Maps.......................... 1 50
Williams (Geo. A.) *Topics in American History.* Cloth, 16mo, pp. 50.... 50
Williams (S. G.) *History of Modern Education.* Cloth. 16mo, pp. 395.... 1 50
Wilson (J. D.) *English Grammar Made Practical.* Cloth, 16mo, pp. 112. 75
——*Elementary English.* Leatherette, 16mo, pp. 67.. 35

Yawger (Rose N.) *How to celebrate Arbor Day.* Paper, 16mo, pp. 14 15
——*The Indian and the Pioneer.* Cloth, 8vo, pp. 335..$3.00 or Two Volumes.... 3 50

Lightning Source UK Ltd.
Milton Keynes UK
UKHW020655061218
333419UK00012B/1444/P

9 781528 566179